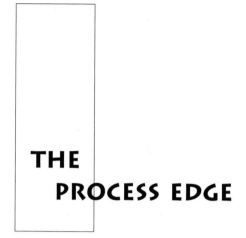

THE
PROCESS EDGE

THE
PROCESS EDGE

CREATING VALUE WHERE IT COUNTS

PETER G. W. KEEN

HARVARD BUSINESS SCHOOL PRESS
BOSTON, MASSACHUSETTS

Library of Congress Cataloging-in-Publication Data

Keen, Peter G. W.
    The process edge : creating value where it counts / Peter G.W.
    Keen.
        p.   cm.
    Includes index.
    ISBN 0-87584-588-6 (alk. paper)
    1. Reengineering (Management)   2. Organizational effectiveness.
    I. Title.
    HD58.87.K44   1997
    658.4'063—dc21   96-48382
                                                               CIP

The paper used in this publication meets the requirements of the American
National Standard for Permanence of Paper for Printed Library Materials
Z39.49-1984.

For my circle of family-friends—they're both of these for me.

And they all contribute to me in my writing through ideas, encouragement, comments, assistance, support and helping me find whatever it is I've mislaid in the last five minutes.

To Sherry, Sara, Chris, Merry, Peggy, Bill, Dale, Jennifer, Russell, and Tracy.

CONTENTS

PREFACE

What I most hope for this book is that its readers will say after reading it, "That's common sense." And that they then add, "Well, now it is." *The Process Edge* is built on proven, practical ideas and tools from many fields. That's what I hope makes its original contribution to management: my search for and synthesis of the best of thought and practice in corporate finance, business process transformation, information technology, economics, and business strategy. Because these fields are very separate—when did you hear a finance expert talk knowledgeably about business process reengineering, for instance, or a total quality management expert speak of the real costs of information technology?—experts in one field rarely recognize how an idea or a technique in other fields can give them new insight.

My career has been in spanning fields, so it's more natural for me to find great ideas in one area and translate them into another. I'm an English literature major who went into the computer field. My doctoral thesis was on the psychology of intuition. I then taught at MIT in organizational behavior and while there wrote my first book on computers. I taught management science at Stanford while writing mainly about organizational change. I returned to

MIT to teach in the management information systems department. My next books were on telecommunications. Then I wrote a series of "every manager's guides" to information technology, business processes, business multimedia, electronic commerce, and the business Internet and intranets. Constantly searching across fields rather than staying within them was how I came across so many separate ideas that needed to be brought together to create something original and useful.

I believe that common sense in research increasingly comes from thinking in multidisciplinary terms, not those of academic departments, just as the new common sense of business processes as competitive opportunity and advantage comes from thinking outside the bounds of functional departments. I define a new common sense idea as one that is obvious fifteen minutes after you hear it but that you wouldn't have thought of fifteen minutes earlier. The common sense I offer in this book is that business processes are financial capital assets or liabilities, to be managed in financial terms. That's not at all part of the common sense today of what I call process movements—total quality management, time-based competition, the learning organization, and others. Nor are the skills and successes of the process movements part of the common sense of finance. The experts who talk about shareholder value don't see these movements as essential contributors to their field.

For years I've been a deep skeptic about business process reengineering. I admired many of the skillful ways of transforming the customer service processes it encouraged, the use of information technology to streamline and coordinate complex administrative work flows, and the powerful new conceptions of competitive strategy it generated. Something didn't make sense, though. I was part of the Cambridge academic-consultant complex that developed reengineering. I knew many of its leaders—Tom Davenport, in many regards the most thoughtful of its originators; Mike Hammer, its leading popularizer; and Jim Champy, both a superb manager and the person credited with coining the term. I shared their belief in information technology as a tool that changes the basics of competitive dynamics in entire industries, opens up new ways of organizing, and makes practical the rethinking, redesigning, and even the intention of business processes.

What concerned me, though, was that the examples intended to show that reengineering transformed organizations didn't illustrate real transformation. Like many people in the Cambridge community, I knew that the firm in one of the two main case examples in Hammer's popular article about obliterating instead of automating processes—an insurance company named Mutual Benefit—had gone broke soon after the article appeared. It didn't surprise me at all that Mutual Benefit wasn't mentioned by name in Hammer and Champy's subsequent book.

As someone who has worked for decades on "people" issues— the dynamics of organizational change, education as the protector of careers when jobs disappear, and cognitive psychology—I disliked the slash-and-kill language of the more evangelistic extremes of the reengineering movement, with talk of breaking legs, shooting the dissenters, and the like. I objected to the very term "reengineering," which implies that people don't matter much; it's fine to talk about reengineering a process, but imagine saying that you're going to reengineer people. That was the tone of much of the early reengineering literature, and it's no surprise that reengineering was soon seen as equivalent to downsizing.

But at the same time, I very much respected the people, ideas, and accomplishments of reengineering. I'd come to respect the precision of total quality management and the deep intellectual and analytic foundations on which it was built over forty years. The literature I read on institutional economics and transaction cost economics, stripped of its often impenetrable prose, showed without doubt that processes are the source of the "firm-specific" special competence that makes the competitive difference far more than does "strategy," products, structure, or industry.

As a writer, teacher, and consultant at senior levels of organizations, I needed to resolve the situation. It was too easy to knock the extremes of reengineering and point to its intellectual and practical inconsistencies and incompleteness. But what did I have to offer instead to my students, clients, and readers, all of whom are increasingly interested in the opportunities and necessities of process change, well aware of the impacts of information technology on the basics of business, and concerned about their careers and jobs in what I call the "cruel economy" of today?

This book is my answer. Developing the ideas in it drew on the support, challenge, and friendship of many people, whom I thank in my Acknowledgments. It was like putting together a giant jigsaw puzzle in which the pieces are turned upside down, revealing no picture. As an unregenerate English literature major who single-handedly protects the U.S. and British bookstores from bankruptcy, my approach to "research" is to read. Since this isn't an academic book, I don't layer the text with the footnotes and references of a scholarly publication. I'd like, though, in this Preface to highlight a few of the books that helped me to fit the pieces together.

Bennett Stewart's 1991 book, *The Quest for Value,* introduced me to economic value-added, a measure of financial planning and performance that has become a new mainstream of corporate finance. Linked to earlier work on shareholder value and economic profits and having some impressive intellectual and academic fore-bears, it provides a wonderfully—"common sensically"—practical framework that changed my understanding of business. It also made me see that the element that has been missing from the fields of information technology and business processes is a reliable economic model. That model had to be based on the economics of capital. Information technology has for too long been evaluated as expense and its capital dynamics overlooked. I'd spotted that in *Shaping the Future,* a book I'd written well before coming across the EVA model; but I hadn't then realized that processes are capital, too. Their true costs, as with IT, are obscured by accounting systems, and their true payoff is either underestimated or overstated by measures such as ROI that ignore the cost of capital and cash flow. I've heard several objections about the details of EVA and the problems of calculating the cost of equity capital, but for me EVA is the necessary conception of the economics of business and for coming to grips with process investment and process payoff. In *The Process Edge,* I don't worry too much about the problems of measuring capital and capital cost, because simply adopting the EVA view and making approximations replaces accounting with reality and gives managers the guide they need for process investment.

The second intellectual path that guided me to the right book-shelves and journals was the one that focused on business processes in terms of coordination rather than as work flows, which has been the predominant conception of reengineering and total quality management. Here, the work of Fernando Flores and his colleagues has been a primary influence on my thinking for two decades now. Fernando is a practical philosopher, widely respected in the hard core of that rarefied field, and a successful entrepreneur and software designer as well. The practicality of his work gives it force for business; the depth and rigor of its intellectual presentation makes it more than a business "methodology" or "software." The foundation of his perspective (on more than just business processes) is that the fundamentals of human life are the coordination of action, and that coordination rests on language, and that language, in turn, rests on requests and promises. I can't do justice to what this means and, indeed, have struggled to grasp its richness. Time and again in working on the frameworks summarized in this book, I'd tell myself that however neat my idea was in a given area, it didn't quite get it. "It" is the ontology of coordination.

What I did get, though, and what I strongly believe the reengineering movement hasn't got, is that process is about coordination, not physical work flows. That recognition helped me address "soft" processes as business assets and include in my frameworks every type of process. Total quality management and reengineering tend to predefine a business process as something their tools can handle. The concept of process as coordination drew me to difficult literature seemingly quite isolated from reality. But the work in economics on transaction cost theory, represented most notably by Oliver Williamson's writing, highlighted the linkage between information technology and business processes as being not so much the impact of IT on streamlining the basics of firms' operations and structure as it is the trade-off between the coordination costs of in-house process management and the transaction costs of going outside and buying from the market.

The last major element in my puzzle piecing was a personal lesson for myself. I grew to realize that my primary concern in developing practical frameworks for management insight and action was the issue of prioritization. A comment I often use in explaining my views on policy as being more important than strategy is, "In a time of constant change, everything becomes a priority. That means that nothing is a priority." The issue is ruthless prioritization, a focus on the small number of areas in which the entire energy and commitment of the organization is focused. I realized that my growing disbelief in the reengineering extremists was misplaced. The process movements have shown how to get a process right. Yes, Mutual Benefit went broke, but that doesn't discredit the superb job it did in transforming a process by reducing the time it took to issue an insurance policy from three weeks to a half day or less. It got the process right but didn't choose the *right process* to get right.

EVA gave me the basis for prioritizing processes. By focusing on the successes of the many process movements and ignoring for the moment their all too frequent choice of the wrong process to get right, I was able to build a menu of process "value builders" from which managers can choose the best way to get a process right, having first selected which ones to get right. I thus provided an economic framework for prioritizing investments and a tool kit for choosing how to implement the investment.

I hope and believe that the result of all my puzzling is a book that is truly useful for managers. I've reviewed how I got to the printed page because I think that my journey is one that businesses everywhere have to take: bringing together the process opportunity, the economic reality, and the information technology. Shareholder value is the driver of our age. Information technology is the enabler of the radical change now becoming the norm. Business processes are the fundamental source of sustainable organizational advantage. People are the most effective coordinators of processes in harmony with and enabled by technology. Common sense says put them all together, and that's what I've done in *The Process Edge.*

ACKNOWLEDGMENTS

Most of my books come from my own ideas or close work with a coauthor or a small group of colleagues. This book is very different, and many people over the past four years have contributed to it. The following are those who have most helped to shape it and to whom I express my sincere thanks and appreciation.

Ellen Knapp, vice chairman of Coopers & Lybrand, first encouraged me to look at the process paradox and develop a way that firms could make reengineering really work. She funded the early work that led to this book and brought together many of Coopers & Lybrand's talent base to challenge, test, and apply the ideas of business process investment. She and I made many presentations of that framework at major conferences.

Stan Raatz, then at Coopers & Lybrand, is among the half dozen or so most powerful thinkers with whom I have worked. Stan helped me move the preliminary frameworks from concept to applicable method, introduced me to complexity theory, and added analytic rigor to my then largely metaphoric ideas.

Lynda Woodman was the colleague who proposed that I look at processes as capital, the single breakthrough in my then-blocked thinking about a topic dominated by conceptions of business processes as work flows. She also introduced me to Bennett Stewart's book on economic value-added, *The Quest for Value,* which gave me the theoretical and empirical grounding for process investment.

Ron Williams of IBM, my good friend for so many years, moved me ahead both by reviewing the first draft of a manuscript that has gone through more versions than any of my previous books as I struggled to crystallize the framework, provided me with a forum in IBM to present it, and continues to be my critic-adviser on its application and on the use of information technology tools as process investment value builders.

Alejandro Garcia and Gelacio Iniguez have for many years now given me a chance to test out new ideas in my work as a consultant to the company they work in, Cemex of Mexico. They provided me with a reality-testing laboratory. Others who helped in this regard were Ian Scott at the World Bank; Ulf Dahlsten and Dag Sehlin, the leaders of Sweden Post; and James Duckworth, head of information systems at Unilever.

I owe thanks, too, to someone I've never met. Bennett Stewart, in *The Quest for Value,* as I mentioned earlier, provides much of the intellectual and empirical grounding for my work on process investment. I've never come across another book like his: a fundamental contribution to business, with enormous implications, that's also fun and funny. Stewart, with his colleague Joel Stern, has made economic value-added the new mainstream of corporate finance. The frameworks I present in *The Process Edge* rest heavily on Stewart's work.

One of the strongest influences on all my work, and on my personal well-being, is Fernando Flores. My only dissatisfaction with this book is that in it I haven't been able to do justice to his depth of insight and astonishing bravura of imagination, precision, business acumen, and knowledge that have shaped and continue to shape my thought and practice. Fernando is the originator of fundamental conceptions in the management and coordination of business processes, and of the central position of people in both processes and process change. Added to his awesome mind are his generosity and humanity. I am proud to call him my teacher as well as my friend.

For any book, a strong and supportive editor is critical. For this book, I was lucky enough to have an editor, Don Cohen, who was far more than this. Thanks to his effort and collaboration, this book is shorter, more cogent, and more well structured.

I am surrounded by people who help me in my everyday work and leverage my time. Writing is extremely time sensitive and time dependent, as well as mood dependent. Jennifer Hunter and Tracy Torregrossa leverage my time and lift my mood. Russell Hunter keeps my computers working and rescues me from the mysteries and minefields of Windows 95.

My wife, Sherry, just makes my life great and makes our Great Falls living room, where I work most of the time (with my laptop computer almost a permanent attachment to my body), a warm, fun, and comfortable place.

Thank you, everyone.

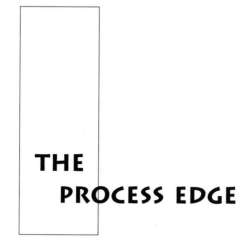

THE
PROCESS EDGE

CHAPTER 1

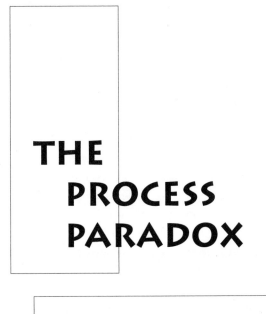

THE
PROCESS
PARADOX

Most of the influential business books and rallying cries of the 1990s have focused on process improvement. Business process reengineering, total quality management (TQM), time-based competition, the team-based organization, and other strategies for business success are all process movements. Reengineering speaks of repairing "broken" processes; TQM highlights the continuous improvement of processes; the team-based organization (as well as the learning organization and the virtual corporation) focuses on achieving more collaborative, flexible, and adaptable business processes. Each of these movements shows how to get a particular kind of process right in a particular way. Most are based on the assumption that a business will improve simply by refocusing on the customer's needs and concerns those operations that were originally designed to match the company's own priorities and structures.

Each process-improvement strategy can lead to notable

1

successes. Firms that undertook process reform have reported radical, not incremental improvements. Dramatic time and cost savings, quality improvements, and staff productivity are commonplace. For example, Harley-Davidson cut delivery time for new motorcycles from 360 days to fewer than 3 by instituting cell manufacturing, a reversal of established manufacturing processes that had been designed to exploit economies of scale, specialization, and volume. The change and resulting improvement helped bring the venerable company back from the brink of extinction. Plains Cotton Cooperative, a cotton broker, reengineered its customer-service processes and increased transactions per employee from 9,000 to 450,000 per year. Toyota exploited TQM and lean production to improve its turnover of work-in-process inventory from 16 times per year to 215. This improvement came *after* Toyota had already become the industry leader in manufacturing processes.

Not so long ago, it would have seemed a stretch to expect to improve a business's efficiency by 10 to 20 percent. In the 1970s, an incremental efficiency improvement of 20 percent was considered a notable news item; two decades later, firms that instituted process reforms were experiencing ten- and twenty-fold increases, and sometimes more than that. Not surprisingly, the transformation of business processes has been big news in the 1990s.

THE PARADOX: BENEFITS ARE NOT VALUE

Not all the news about process transformation has been good, however. Many firms have found that even dramatic levels of process improvement often don't translate into better business performance. In fact, they may not even prevent disaster, let alone bring success. Mutual Benefit, the insurance firm whose success in cutting the time it took to issue a policy from around three weeks to three hours in effect launched the business process reengineering movement, fell into insolvency, and was taken over by regulators a few months after the influential article lauding its achievement appeared in print. Both IBM Corp. and General Motors Corp. received the Baldrige Award, the most prestigious prize for business quality in the United States, at the very time they were falling into disarray. Another Baldrige winner, Florida Power and Light, was one of the darlings of the TQM movement, cutting the average annual per-customer power outage from seven days to one-half day. While doing so, however, it created a new bureaucracy, upset its customers, and infuriated regulators.

These are all examples of the *process paradox,* the startling fact that businesses can decline and even fail at the same time that process reform is dramatically improving efficiency by saving the company time and money and improving product quality and customer service. The phenomenon is described in an article that ought to alarm any firm that has initiated programs to transform business processes:

> In all too many companies, reengineering has been not only a great success but also a great failure. After months, even years, of careful redesign, these companies achieve dramatic improvements in individual processes only to watch overall results decline. By now, paradoxical outcomes of this kind have become almost commonplace. A computer company reengineers its finance department, reducing process costs by 34%—yet operating income stalls. An insurer cuts claims processing time by 44%—yet profits drop. Managers proclaim a 20% cost reduction, a 25% quality improvement—yet in the same period business-unit costs increase and profits decline.[1]

This process paradox is similar to the productivity paradox that has been debated for a decade in relation to information technology (IT). Coined by economist Stephen Roach, the term *productivity paradox* refers to the fact that, despite the powerful market and service innovations created by computers and telecommunications in the early 1980s, there is no evidence that investment in IT has had *any* effect on overall productivity in financial services. Although it has become commonplace to associate IT with a "competitive advantage," Roach has pointed out that the $100 billion U.S. firms invested in IT in the 1980s (tripling capital investment per worker in ten years) left productivity essentially unchanged.[2] Study after study confirmed Roach's contention that there was no correlation between a firm's level of IT spending and its business performance.

The productivity paradox has caused many firms to look more carefully and skeptically at their investments in IT: $100 billion is a lot of money to waste. The process paradox similarly raises serious questions about reengineering and other process strategies. The negative results just described threaten the credibility of all process reforms and ask whether pursuing competitive innovation and organizational transformation through business processes is an expensive mistake. There are now as many articles attacking reengineering as there were ones praising it a short time ago. One of the originators of the reengineering concept and the coauthor of a widely read book on the subject said in late 1995 that reengineering had become a disaster.

Given this bleak assessment, we must inevitably ask, Is process reform dead? I believe that it is not. The companies that have suffered from the process paradox—those whose process-reform success was met by business stagnation or failure—clearly got some process right. But that is much different from getting the *right* process right. Over the past decade, firms have learned a lot—often painfully—about how to design and implement TQM programs, reengineer work flows, build teams, and outsource tasks. The results of their efforts indicate that they have learned far less about how to pick the right processes to invest in.

Stephen Roach now says that the productivity paradox that raised doubts about IT investments has been resolved by shifting IT's focus from back-office and administrative functions to those that directly provide value to customers. Studies now show a strong correlation between this kind of IT investment and corporate competitiveness. It has taken almost a decade to arrive at this more productive IT priority. Process movements point in the right direction, but they tend to focus on processes that—however dramatically they are improved, reengineered, transformed, downsized, or streamlined—do not substantially affect the capabilities that most influence a firm's strategic future. Businesses cannot afford to wait a decade to learn how to figure out what their process-reform priorities should be. They need to make the right choices now. Helping them to do so is the aim of *The Process Edge*. In this book I present an economic framework for deciding which business processes are worth investing in and provide the tools needed to apply it to today's corporations. The framework and the tools are based on two key concepts: the *salience* of a process, or its relative importance to a firm, and the *worth* of a process, or the economic value it generates. I consider these concepts in detail later. First, though, I need to explain why business process reform is as important as ever.

THE OLD IN THE NEW

Process movement leaders have made much of the newness of process reform. A book on TQM begins, "This book is about a revolution." The leader of the reengineering movement has claimed that it is his personal mission to reverse the history of the industrial revolution. Process movement literature is full of claims of originality that, by implication at least, criticize traditional management strategies, tools, skills, and attitudes. These claims are probably counterproductive, creating the impression that process reform is a fad whose day has come and may already have gone. In fact, process thinking sharpens and extends much of what is old. It may use new terminology, but its concepts have deep roots in the literature on institutional economics, in the long tradition of industrial engineering and socio-technical change, and in the histories of companies that have been successful for half a century or more. Its principles are well-grounded in historical trends and have been proven over time.

James Utterback's work shows that process improvement has been intrinsic to business success for centuries.[3] Mary Parker Follett's influential writings of the 1920s called for the same cross-functional organization that process-reform gurus have labeled "revolutionary."[4] And here is Peter Drucker writing on employee empowerment—a cornerstone of process movements—in 1959, thirty years before it was touted as a new idea:

> The business enterprise of today is no longer an organization in which there are a handful of bosses at the top who make all the

decisions while the workers carry out the orders. It is primarily an organization of highly-specialized knowledge workers exercising autonomous, responsible judgment. And every one of them—whether manager or individual expert contributor—constantly makes truly entrepreneurial decisions, that is, decisions which affect the economic characteristics of the entire enterprise.[5]

These examples don't discredit process reform; they support it. The staying power of process movement ideas is a much more convincing indicator of their lasting value than their supposed originality. My approach to process improvement is this: ignore the ideology and buzzwords and instead look at the basics of business evolution that this popular jargon builds on and sometimes hides.

THE PROCESS ADVANTAGE

There are four main reasons for viewing business process improvement as a key to sustainable competitive advantage in today's economy—and the failure to improve the appropriate processes as a corresponding disadvantage.

ORGANIZATIONAL PLASTICITY

Organizations are far less rigid than they were believed to be during the stable and relatively benign competitive environment of the 1950s through the 1970s. The literature on organizational change from that period and into the 1980s stressed the difficulty of making more than incremental improvements in processes. Change was seen as an occasional exception to the rule. The status quo needed to be carefully "unfrozen," and change had to be even more carefully "managed," often with the help of "process consultants." When change happened at all, a new stability had to be ensured through "refreezing" the organization's roles, relationships, structures, and incentives. Hardly a single instance of successful radical or transformational change is reported in almost thirty years of change management literature. The process writers then emphasized the need for well-planned, incremental change over time. Their socio-technical view was that processes are relatively fixed and dominated by a human element whose resistance to change has to be respected.

The many instances of radical process improvement that mark the 1990s prove that dramatic change is far more possible than the socio-technical literature assumed and that organizations are more adaptable—more *plastic*—than previously believed. Although the process paradox shows that aggressive process improvement is not always a business advantage, radical improvement nonetheless changes the terms of business competition and requires entire industries to catch up to the leaders. If competitors are more or less equally sluggish, there is little advantage or disadvantage in being slightly faster or slower. For instance, when it took the life insurance industry an average of twenty-four days to issue a policy, there was no significant competitive difference between the company that needed twenty-eight days and the one that did the job in twenty. But when Mutual Benefit cut the time to three *hours,* the competitive rules changed. The firms that continued to carry the staff, overhead, and other costs associated with a twenty-four-day process fell hopelessly behind on service and costs. They had to change to survive. So the plasticity of firms makes change through process reform essential across whole industries.

The pattern of radical changes being forced on the pack by breakaway players is apparent in the auto industry. Detroit automakers had set their own manufacturing pace and priorities for more than fifty years, but these rules were drastically changed in the 1970s, when Toyota cut years from the seven it typically took American companies to design and launch new car models *and* set new standards for quality. The historically rigid U.S. industry had to become plastic to bridge the production gap opened up by Toyota. Chrysler Corp., for example, cut its new-model cycle in the 1980s from fifty-nine months to thirty-nine months for its LH truck line and thirty-one months for its successful Neon models in the 1990s.

Similarly, Kmart Corp.'s strategic goals have been set by Wal-Mart Stores, which put the secure but complacent discount store into a catch-up position in which it has had to look for radical solutions to its growing process problems. Wal-Mart's process strengths in streamlining its supply chain to get the right goods on the right shelf at the right time accentuated Kmart's comparative weakness here. The customers saw the gap. Southwest Airlines established the terms of competition for United Airlines, Delta Air Lines, and Continental Airlines. Its profitability edge was built on process advantages, not on better aircraft. It consistently earned more per passenger mile than the others, at lower prices to customers, and forced its rivals to rethink the basics of their service, staffing, and culture. When the gaps in productivity and performance are relatively narrow, incremental improvement works; when they are wide, incrementalism ceases to be an option. Change drives change.

The gap in operating capabilities between industry leaders and their competitors is currently very high, as measured by profits and sales per employee, two indicators of process capability. So the pace of change is likely to accelerate for the rest of the 1990s, and the need for business process improvement will be greater than ever. Table 1-1 shows some examples, reported by *Forbes* in its survey of industries published in April 1995.

The gaps between the leader and the median performer in Table 1-1 average more than 50 percent. The mere existence of comparable large gaps in so many industries demonstrates the truth of organizational plasticity, as so many different businesses have changed so dramatically and pulled away from their competitors. The conventional wisdom about the limits of change has to give way to the opportunity and necessity of change. The *Forbes* figures show that the median firm must improve by half or more in the same market with the same customer base, products, access to technology, and opportunities. This requirement underlies the philosophy of reengineering and its enthusiastic reception.

THE CRUEL ECONOMY AND THE CHANGING NATURE OF CHANGE

It is no secret that we live in era of relentless competition, eroding margins, overcapacity, gradual but continuing global deregulation, increasing customer power and sophistication, and accelerating business cycles. Quality and service, once the hallmarks of market leaders, are now basic requirements. Businesses today can

TABLE 1-1

SOME INDUSTRY LEADERS' SALES AND PROFITS, APRIL 1995 (IN $000S PER EMPLOYEE)

INDUSTRY MEDIAN	Sales	Profits	INDUSTRY LEADER	Sales	Profits
Advertising and publishing	134	13	Reader's Digest	438	31
Airlines	102	2	Southwest Airlines	162	11
Brokerage	426	15	Merrill Lynch & Co.	1044	44
Cars and trucks	380	16	Chrysler Corp.	466	33
Car parts	146	7	Genuine Parts	232	14
Chemicals	279	21	Union Carbide	388	31
Computer peripherals	284	27	Cisco	655	139
Computer software	224	31	Microsoft Corp.	339	84
Computer systems	331	19	Compaq Computer Corp.	872	70
Department stores	124	4	May Department Stores	143	9
Drug and discount	139	2	Walgreen's	159	7
International banks	319	40	J. P. Morgan & Co.	739	75
Oil	980	36	Exxon Corp.	1126	58
Personal products	174	13	Clorox Co.	393	39
Regional banks	175	24	Collective BNCP	358	67
Shipping	110	2	American Presidential	516	14
Telecommunications	189	19	Citizens	254	40

SOURCE: *Forbes,* 23 April, 1995, 17.

no longer be content to find an edge; they must find and sustain *the* edge. No firm is safe today, no matter how successful or even dominant it has been in the past.

Who would have believed, in 1980, that the disaster cases of the early 1990s would include IBM, Sears Roebuck & Co., General Motors, Citibank, and Digital Equipment Corp.; that Bloomingdale's and Macy's would file for Chapter 11 bankruptcy; and that American Airlines would actively look to get out of the airline business? By 1985, thirty years after the Fortune 500 was first defined, 238 of the firms on the initial list had disappeared as independent entities, an average of 8 a year. Between 1985 and 1990, another 143 were gone, disappearing at a rate of almost 30 per year. Of the 43 companies identified by Tom Peters and Robert Waterman as models for the new business age in their 1984 book, *In Search of Excellence,* only 12 remain in good shape; some have been disasters. Only 6 of the top 20 discount chains of 1980 were still in business in 1990. In every industry in which deregulation and technology have changed the basis of competition, 50 percent of the firms trying to compete in traditional modes have declined dramatically or disappeared within a decade. Some of the casualties were once market leaders: TWA, Eastern Airlines, and Pan Am; retailers Macy's and Bloomingdale's; and computer companies including Wang, Data General, and Unisys, as well as IBM and Digital. Managers who previously took for granted that their firm's size, products, advertising, distribution systems, and other assets ensured that they would stay in business, riding out bad times and benefiting from booms, now know that their apparently unassailable advantages can quickly disappear.

Change has become the norm, not the exception. The old principles of change management, which stressed incrementalism, are inadequate to respond to the waves of change that characterize almost every business environment. Although TQM still adheres to many of these principles, numerous commentators and managers challenge their contemporary usefulness. Paul O'Neil, the chairman of Alcoa, summarizes the change in attitude:

> I believe we have made a major mistake in our advocacy of continuous improvement. Let me explain what I mean. Continuous improvement is exactly the right idea if you are the world leader in everything you do. It is a terrible idea if you are lagging in the world leadership benchmark. It is probably a disastrous idea if you are far behind the world standard. . . . [W]e need rapid, quantum-leap improvement. We cannot be satisfied to lay out a plan that will move us toward the existing world standard over some protracted period of time—say 1995 to 2000—because if we accept such a plan, we will never be the world leader.[6]

Transformation, not incrementalism, describes the new agenda for change. Many process movements focus on how to encourage flexibility, learning, and collaboration—a new kind of organizational plasticity. Every major development in management thought and practice is pushing toward organizational processes that subordinate tightness of procedures and efficiency to flexibility and adaptability so that the challenges of change can be met. The more uncertain and volatile the near-term environment of a firm, the more important a fast and flexible response becomes, not so much to generate business value directly but to enable the organization to seize opportunities to do so. Companies cannot tinker their way into the future but must be ready to move boldly.

Change was once seen as an issue of organizational structure, and structure and strategy were assumed to be interdependent, with structure following strategy. This view reflected a belief in the possibility of controlling both the firm and its environment, of creating a long-term structure and a strategy that would need only fine-tuning in the future. The language of management was the language of control: span of control, management-control systems, forecasting, synergy, exception reporting, management by objective. The language of business is now about how to plan when you can't predict, how to be adaptable, and how to handle the discontinuities of change. Organizational change is now process- rather than structure-centered. Managers cannot control their business environments or even predict what they will be like in a few years. Rather than be architects of structures and strategies that may be made irrelevant or even obliterated by the next tidal wave of change, they focus on how work is done, on the process reforms that promise the flexibility needed to meet unforeseen challenges and take advantage of unexpected opportunities.

DYNAMIC CAPABILITIES

Plasticity and the acceleration of change reflect the market forces that have given rise to business process movements in the 1990s. Another reason for the importance of these movements—less visible but no less significant—is their contribution to the dynamic capabilities of firms. Economists think of dynamic capabilities as firm-specific assets, a distinctive competence defined as "a set of differentiated skills, complementary assets and organizational routines which together allow a firm to coordinate a particular set of activities in a way that provides the basis for competitive advantage in a particular market or markets."[7] Developing this competence requires "investment in specialized information, education and training, physical assets and systems for coordination and integration, and incentives."[8]

The importance of dynamic capabilities was made clear by studies showing that the differences among profits of companies within industries are greater than those among companies across industries. The *Forbes* figures in Table 1-1 indicate the typical range. A 1988 study of eighteen manufacturing plants in the air-conditioning industry showed immense differences in performance from plant to plant even though market conditions, products, and manufacturing technology were similar across the board. The authors ascribe these differences to "organizational routines affecting coordination"—in other words, to process differences.

The fact that performance variations within industries are greater than those across industries challenges the industry-centered view of profitability. Jeffrey Pfeffer states the case well in *Competitive Advantage through People*:

> Suppose that in 1972, someone asked you to pick five companies that would provide the greatest return to stockholders over the next 20 years. . . . Conventional wisdom then (and even now) would have you begin by selecting the right industries. After all, "not all industries offer equal opportunity for sustained profitability, and the inherent profitability of its industry is one essential ingredient in determining the profitability of a firm."[9]

Pfeffer quotes from Michael Porter's *Five Forces of Industry Competition*, which developed an influential model of corporate strategy. Pfeffer then identifies, in reverse order, the five firms that returned the greatest profits to stockholders: Plenum Publishing (16,000 percent), Circuit City, Tyson Foods, Wal-Mart, and Southwest Airlines (nearly 22,000 percent). Pfeffer continues:

> During this period, these industries (retailing, airlines, publishing, and food processing) were characterized by massive competition and horrendous losses, widespread bankruptcy, virtually no

barriers to entry (for airlines after 1978), little unique or proprietary technology, and many substitute products and services. And in 1972, none of these firms was (and some are still not) the market-share leader, enjoying economies of scale from moving down the learning curve.[10]

Like the economists mentioned earlier, Pfeffer argues that competitive advantage today comes from developing firm-specific capabilities built on the processes by which a company manages its people and relationships and through which it builds and rewards skills. He notes that this is a source of success "that is difficult to duplicate and consequently is sustainable over time." Again, business processes (and therefore business process improvement) are at the heart of this source of competitive advantage.

COORDINATION AND TRANSACTION COSTS AND THE ROLE OF IT

Business processes are coordinated activities that involve people, procedures, and technology. MIT's Tom Malone, a leader in the process field, calls the intellectual underpinning of his work "coordination theory."[11] Fernando Flores, whose research has led to powerful practical tools for process transformation, argues that the core of business processes is coordination through language.[12] Coordination underlies the increasingly influential field of transaction-cost economics, which addresses the question of which aspects of their operations firms should handle internally (incurring coordination costs) and which they should obtain from outside markets (incurring transaction costs). Transaction-cost economics suggests that coordination and transaction costs are the basis of how organizations operate.

This concept was first explored by British economist Ronald Coase in a paper published in 1937 (he also won the Nobel prize for the theory, more than forty years later).[13] Coase asked why firms exist at all and zeroed in on how they decide which aspects of their operations to handle internally (coordination) and which to buy (transactions) as the very foundation of the organization. Although transaction-cost economics does not use the term "outsourcing," the make-or-buy decision is a central element of the theory; the firm and the market are seen as alternative locations for carrying out the very same activities. Much of the work that is coordinated is linked to firm-specific assets. Toyota, for example, keeps the skill- and culture-dependent capabilities needed to develop new car models in house. At the same time, it outsources the manufacture of most components. Chrysler and the Ford Motor Co. have followed Toyota's lead by outsourcing component manufacture, increasing transactions costs, and reducing coordination costs—and improving their performance and profit margins in the process. Firms that sell a product or a service can often provide it more efficiently than an internal department. Even a giant organization would find it hard to deliver small packages more cheaply than Federal Express and United Parcel Service, so it makes more sense to pay them to do so than to build an internal capacity to perform the same task.

Obviously, any major change in coordination costs will affect make-or-buy decisions. Information technology is bringing about just such a change. By creating new ways of overcoming the barriers of physical distance and dramatically reducing the number of process steps and personnel, IT can radically lower coordination costs and provide opportunities to develop new, internal processes that are in fact firm-specific assets. Recent innovations in IT have, for instance, made it possible for individual case managers to handle entire customer-service transactions. That is how Mutual Benefit reengineered its policy-issuing procedures and reduced the time required from weeks to hours.

Information technology is now as much about coordination as about information. Electronic data interchange, which links intercompany ordering, delivery, and payment systems; groupware, which allows people to work collaboratively at a distance; and customer self-service through automated teller machines (ATMs) are all examples of coordination technology in practice. The virtual corporation exploits coordination technology to handle outside relationships and seize transaction-cost opportunities without having to build a complex internal organization.

Ongoing technological innovation and technology costs that drop at rates of up to 40 percent a year mean that IT will continue to open up new opportunities for fundamental process improvement. *The Corporation of the 1990s* indicates the breadth of these opportunities:

> This change in the economics and functionality of coordination fundamentally alters all the tasks in an organization that have to do with coordinating the organization's delivery of products and services to its customers and the actual production of such goods and services. To the extent that an organization's structure is determined by its coordinative needs, it too is subject to potential change.[14]

BUSINESS PROCESS INVESTMENT

All of these powerful factors—organizational plasticity, the cruel economy and the changing nature of change, dynamic capabilities, and the effect of IT on crucially important coordination and transactions costs—make the kinds of fundamental improvements promised by process movements both possible and obligatory. In an era of intense competition and rapid change, when trying to protect the status quo is a losing proposition, transforming the corporation is not just a dream but an urgent necessity. Reengineering, outsourcing, the learning organization, and TQM have become part of management's everyday vocabulary because they offer ways to make the fundamental improvements that must be made if businesses are to survive and thrive. The disillusionment that ensues when results don't match the exaggerated claims made by some process zealots should not be allowed to obscure the primary importance of process reform. As I have suggested, the process paradox that causes some businesses to decline even as some of their processes improve is caused by investing in the wrong processes, not any by inherent fallacy in process improvement.

SALIENCE AND WORTH

The firm that piles change program on change program in the hope of somehow getting ahead of its competitors is not only unlikely to achieve that goal but will also waste its financial and human resources on repeated disruptive and disappointing initiatives. The process *opportunity* is to take charge of change by focusing attention, money, and human resources on a small number of major opportunities. In other words, the firm should invest only in the processes that make a difference. The process *problem,* for which I offer practical guides for action, is how to identify these processes.

SALIENCE. The word *salience* suggests standing out from the general surface, being prominent; salient processes are the most prominent ones. They are the processes that relate most directly to the firm's identity—those that visibly differentiate it from its competitors—and the priority activities that keep the engine of everyday competitive performance running. Much of the process paradox can be explained by the fact that firms have invested in processes that were not critical to their success. Processes were improved, sometimes dramatically, but they were not the salient ones. Key processes went on unexamined, some even suffering from the attention given to less important ones, so the change program succeeded but the firm succumbed.

WORTH. Processes that return more money to the firm than they cost in terms of capital are assets; processes that cost more than they return are liabilities. The worth of a process is the economic value it adds to a firm. A process may be radically improved, providing impressive, measurable benefits, but benefits are not value. If the process costs more than it earns, it is draining the firm's value, not increasing it. Some of the process paradox is due to investment in processes without a meaningful accounting of their true cost and therefore a lack of understanding that the benefits of reform may not be worth what is paid for them. Think about the reengineering project that streamlines and accelerates an administrative process that is, in terms of worth, a process liability. It's still a liability after the reengineering.

Even more common are projects that generate an apparent high return on investment or direct cost savings. The figures may appear attractive, but they overlook the dynamics of capital—accumulated and ongoing cost; how much capital is tied up by the process; the many hidden capital costs such as for training, support, existing computer systems and others; and the investment generator's real contribution to cash flow. As I discuss a few pages on, "value" means cash flow return, not accounting "paper profits."

It is commonsensical that business processes differ from one another in their importance to a firm's success and future opportunities, and that investing in key processes is more likely to help the firm thrive than investing in lesser ones. It is also clear that activities that add to a firm's value are more desirable than those that drain it, so a reasonable investment is one that promises to return more than it costs. It is therefore obvious that making reasonable investments in key processes is the secret of successful process reform. So why can it be so difficult to determine what those key processes are and what levels of investment are appropriate? Two potential problems lie in defining process too narrowly and making a faulty accounting of what it costs.

MORE THAN WORK FLOW

Influential process movement literature defines *process* as "a collection of activities that takes one or more inputs and creates an output that is of value to the customer," "a structured, measured set of activities designed to produce a specified output for a particular customer or market," or "a specific ordering of work activities across time and space, with a beginning, an end, and clearly identified inputs and outputs." This idea of processes as work flows— with clearly definable inputs and outputs and discrete tasks that follow and depend on one another in a clear succession—comes from the tradition of industrial engineering (as the term *reengineering* suggests). A work flow is only one kind of process, though. The process-as-work flow definition excludes many processes that have no clear inputs, flows, and outputs. Some of these processes— such as those governing management succession, acquisitions, manager-staff relations, management development, and incentives and promotions—have as much or more impact on a firm's success than the manufacturing and customer-service processes that are usually the target of process investment initiatives.

The fascinating and vivid *Comeback: The Fall and Rise of the American Auto Industry* provides a clear example.[15] It describes how Chrysler's roller-coaster years of disaster followed by success followed by disaster (followed most recently by success) stemmed to a significant degree from the lack of a coherent management succession process. Efforts to improve product quality and to reengineer manufacturing were offset by the company's succession problems. The book contrasts Chrysler's difficulties with Honda's skill at ensuring smooth leadership transitions that enhanced its overall management effectiveness. Problems created by Chrysler's faulty leadership succession process include the loss of several outstanding executives and the influence that Lee Iacocca's forced retirement may have had on his decision to join with Kirk Kerkorian in launching a hostile $22.8 billion takeover bid in 1995.

Chrysler has also been badly hurt by its acquisition decisions, diversifying ineffectually and paying steep premiums for companies that failed to justify the investment. In 1979, for instance, it sold its entire European operations, including expensive British and French acquisitions, for one dollar. Several Japanese firms, famous for the excellence of their manufacturing processes and exemplars of the TQM movement, have shown that their acquisition processes were not of comparable quality. In mid-1995, consumer electronics maker Pioneer wrote off $90 million in losses from its investments in Hollywood and in a U.S. software firm, and Matsushita Electric Industrial sold off its holdings in MCA, the huge entertainment company. A year earlier, Sony had written off $250 million of its investment in Columbia Pictures. These acquisitions were not necessarily bad choices, but the Japanese owners managed the U.S. entertainment companies in the same way that they managed their domestic manufacturing firms, without considering that very different processes might be needed for these very different firms. Sony's acquisition process lacked effective supporting management processes for handling the transition, meshing cultures, and developing shared understanding. When the head of Sony's American operations resigned in December 1995, he attributed his departure specifically to this process problem.

Many firms have effective processes for meshing cultures. The Anglo-Dutch giants Unilever and Shell Oil Co. demonstrate the

Dutch cultural sensitivity in formal organizational, management development, and reward processes that address exactly the issues Sony ignored. Unilever maintains two head offices—one in London and one in Rotterdam—for this reason. Its selection, training, and rotation of managers is designed to ensure a fit, not a conflict, between its many employed nationalities. Indeed, one cannot understand Unilever's strategy and organization without understanding these processes.

Defining processes as work flow can cause management to ignore other processes that may be in dire need of improvement. Even when succession, acquisition, and cultural processes are recognized as such, the engineering bias of process movements may not see these "soft" processes—which lack obvious inputs, outputs, and flow patterns—as amenable to systematic reform. I believe that they can and should be subject to investment and improvement. To counter the myopia of the work flow definition, I suggest a new definition: "A process is any work that meets these four criteria: it is recurrent; it affects some aspect of organizational capabilities; it can be accomplished in different ways that make a difference to the contribution it generates in terms of cost, value, service, or quality; and it involves coordination." This definition embraces recurrent processes as diverse as management succession and computer assembly; its idea of coordination includes both the sequencing of manufacturing steps and the back-and-forth interactions between business team members.

PROCESS AS CAPITAL

Traditional accounting treats business processes as expenses. This view, which I call "the accounting trap," leads to two serious problems. First, it can cause firms to underestimate the true cost of processes—the total amount of capital tied up in making a process happen and continue to happen. As a result, a company may imagine that a particular process is successful when it actually costs more in capital than it earns in contribution to cash flow. Second, seeing processes as expenses ignores the fact that, like research and design (also considered as expenses by accounting), they can be assets generative of future value. *The Process Edge* views business processes as financial capital. Not only do they *tie up* capital, and therefore represent capital investment, but in many instances they *are* the business's main capital—its assets and liabilities, its value.

Even though processes don't appear on the balance sheet as such, managers intuitively recognize that they are assets, not expenses. An article making the case for a new type of financial controller to monitor and analyze "off-balance-sheet resources" quotes a survey of sixty executives who were asked to list their firms' top three resources.[16] Only five of the sixty mentioned traditional balance-sheet assets such as cash, facilities, and equipment. The resources most frequently named were intangibles like quality of personnel and management, corporate culture, distribution system, brand equity, technology, and knowledge. These results not only show how easy it is for accounting to miss the real assets of a company; they highlight just how closely factors such as culture, distribution, and technology are linked to process capabilities.

Uncovering the direct link between business processes and capital investment is a principal goal of this book. Process investment represents a reallocation of a firm's financial capital. A growing proportion of existing and new capital investments goes to processes that have significant influence over whether a firm creates or erodes wealth, and over whether it builds a solid foundation for future opportunity and success. Unfortunately, as the process paradox shows, a growing portion of investments too often goes to processes that don't make a real contribution to performance. Getting the right process right means using capital to build wealth; getting the wrong one right casts the illusion of success but cracks the foundation—or fails to build it. Reduced costs, enhanced service, or increased profits translate to value only if they generate a cash flow that exceeds the amount of capital used to achieve those benefits.

ECONOMIC VALUE-ADDED: BEYOND PAPER PROFITS

This commonsensical idea is formalized in the relatively new mainstream of corporate finance called *economic value-added* (EVA). Quite simply, EVA is the after-tax cash flow a firm derives from its invested capital less the cost of that capital. EVA represents what Warren Buffet calls "owners' earnings," as opposed to paper profits. A key finding of the theorists who developed EVA is that reported profits and earnings per share do not correlate to share-holder value (in terms of the total market value of the firm), but EVA does—strongly. Peter Drucker, so often among the first to articulate important new business ideas, asserts bluntly that when a firm consistently fails to generate after-tax cash flow larger than the cost of the capital provided by its shareholders, it destroys both its capital and shareholder value.[17]

An article in *Fortune* makes explicit the connection between intangibles such as processes and EVA:

> How much capital is tied up in your operations? Even if you don't know the answer, you know what it consists of: what you paid for real estate, machines, vehicles and the like, plus working capital. But proponents of EVA say there's more. What about the money your company spends on R&D? On employee training? Those are investments meant to pay off for years, but accounting rules say you can't treat them that way; you have to call them expenses, like the amounts you spend on electricity. EVA proponents say forget the accounting rules. For internal purposes, call these things what they are: capital investments. No one can say what their useful life is, so make your best guess—say five years. It's truer than calling them expenses.[18]

Because business processes are a substantial, though largely hidden part of a firm's total capital, EVA is an essential tool for business process investment; it is the only way to determine whether a particular process is an asset or a liability. Some of the companies I discuss later—notably, PepsiCo, Inc., CSX, and AT&T Corp.—report major improvements in resource allocation to processes as a direct result of adopting EVA.

RESOLVING THE PROCESS PARADOX

I have suggested most of the business principles that underlie the business process investment concept. To sum up:

- Business processes are assets and liabilities, part of the firm's capital base.
- Sustainable competitive advantage rests on the effective use of capital.
- Most approaches to process innovation and reengineering overlook the nature of processes as real capital.
- Processes are not just work flows.
- Some processes are more important to a firm than others (salience).
- Economic value-added is the necessary measure of process pay-off (worth).
- Benefits are not the same as value.

Applying these principles helps managers to resolve the process paradox. In Chapter 2, I describe the worth/salience matrix, an essential analytic tool that offers a clear graphic representation of the relative importance and value of a firm's processes.

Not all processes should be improved in the same way. Many offer opportunities to create EVA, but only if they are handled appropriately. In the chapters that follow, I discuss practical ways to increase process assets and decrease process liabilities. These options, which I call "process value builders," range from abandoning unnecessary processes to streamlining and outsourcing to turning a process into a product and finding ways to develop a supposedly minor process into one that is central to a firm's identity and value. Some process value builder choices are low cost and low risk. Others, especially radical efforts to transform major areas of a business, demand huge and risky capital investment that may or may not yield comparably huge returns.

Investment is always an issue of potential risk versus potential return. Given the complexity and competitiveness of today's economic environment, *The Process Edge* cannot guarantee success. It does, however, provide tools for a purposeful analysis of process investment opportunities and for balancing risk and return. Worth and salience provide a way of linking business processes to corporate strategy and corporate finance. Value builders show how to apply the best and most appropriate process movement tools to the processes that have the greatest potential to add economic value. Together they offer a clear, rigorous, flexible approach to investment decisions that have too often been marred either by vagueness about what was being spent and gained or by a doctrinaire application of the one "true" process answer to every process problem.

CHAPTER 2

THE SALIENCE/WORTH MATRIX

THE SALIENCE/WORTH MATRIX IS THE BASIC ANALYTICAL TOOL for determining which processes most deserve attention and investment. The matrix (see Figure 2-1) clearly shows a given process's importance to a firm and whether it adds or drains value. The process's position in the matrix allows managers to decide what (if anything) should be done to change it.

The worth axis is essentially self-explanatory. Although determining a process's worth is not always simple, the basic principle is: any process that returns more money to the firm than it costs is an asset. A process that costs more than it returns is a liability. (Chapter 4 addresses some of the practical complexities of determining worth.) The four categories on the salience axis are a bit more complicated. I'll describe them in order of importance.

An *identity* process is one that defines the company for itself, its customers, and its investors. It differentiates a firm from its competitors and is at the heart of the firm's success. For instance,

FIGURE 2-1

THE SALIENCE/WORTH MATRIX

SALIENCE	WORTH	
	ASSETS	LIABILITIES
Identity		
Priority		
Background		
Mandated		

Federal Express's reliability defines the company and is the source of its success: think of Federal Express and you think of guaranteed on-time delivery. McDonald's is known for speedy, consistent food preparation, and customer loyalty is based on an expectation of that consistency. Nearly every product and management decision at McDonald's is made to support that essential identity process. The mail-order and delivery systems for which Dell Computer Corp. is known are also identity processes.

Priority processes are the engine of corporate effectiveness. They strongly influence how well identity processes are carried out and how a firm stands relative to its competition. For Federal Express, processes related to airplane operations are priority. These are not identity processes, as customers don't think of Federal Express as an airline and don't care about the specifics of flight schedules and airplane maintenance. Priority processes tend to be invisible to the customer (Federal Express picks up your package today and delivers it tomorrow), but when they fail the problems are visible and immediate (the package did not arrive on time because the plane couldn't take off). For McDonald's, food-supply management is a priority process. Customers think of McDonald's as a family restaurant, not a food distributor. They will not give food-supply management a thought unless the process breaks down, and they discover they can't get fries with their Big Macs.

Background processes are a necessary support to daily operations. Many administrative and overhead functions are background processes. For Federal Express, McDonald's, and numerous other companies, payroll processing is background. For most companies, office management, document management, accounting, and many other common administrative processes are background. They are often the core of daily operations, but it is a mistake to allow their visibility to make them the main target for management attention and capital investment, because improving them rarely generates much EVA. Such information technology tools as groupware are naturally suited to streamlining processes with well-defined flows, numerous forms, and photocopying and other procedures, so it's not at all surprising that, in my experience, around 75 percent of firms' reengineering targets are these background liability processes.

Mandated processes are those a company carries out only because it is legally required to do so. Regulatory reporting and filing tax returns are obvious examples. Mandated processes are almost always liability processes; they rarely create economic value. The capital tied up in these processes can be considerable. Chrysler's corporate federal income tax forms stack up more than eight feet high. Regulatory reporting consumes the full-time effort of whole departments in many companies. In industries such as workers' compensation insurance, pharmaceuticals, and securities trading, mandated processes represent a sizable proportion of total costs; the capital tied up in regulation-generated bureaucracy drains EVA.

A salience category that does not appear in the matrix is *folklore*—processes that are carried out only because they have been in the past. As they serve no purpose and create no economic value, they are not part of the matrix; they are always liabilities and should be abandoned when discovered.

Folklore processes may be difficult to spot because they are so deeply embedded in the fabric of a firm that no one questions them. A consulting firm studying a large company's information systems came across a monthly report in 1994 that was expensive to generate but was not used by any managers. The consultants discovered that it had been created ten years before for an executive who died only six months after it first appeared. It had been dutifully and pointlessly produced ever since.

A common folklore process in many firms is the cumbersome purchase-approval procedure for buying software and computer accessories. It was developed when the price of such items could easily run to six figures, and it has been retained even though those costs have dropped to three figures or even two.

I can generally attest to the staying power of folklore processes. As a schoolboy in England in the late 1950s, I took part in the British equivalent of ROTC training in American colleges. During my training, I spent one year as part of a six-member team, learning the procedures, timing, and teamwork needed to fire anti-aircraft guns. Part of the sequence required two members of the team to move ten yards behind the forty-foot gun and kneel. I later learned that, in the 1970s, the British army finally asked what essential purpose the retreat-and-kneel move served. A veteran of the Boer Wars provided the answer: to hold the horses that moved the guns so that they would not panic and flee.

Putting the Matrix to Work: Dell and Compaq

In the early 1990s, Dell Computer transformed personal computer retailing by creating a process, rather than a product, advantage. The computers it sold were not notably different from those of its competitors, but Dell invented a new way of selling them. Using phone ordering, customized assembly, and package delivery services like UPS for distribution, it offered customers superior pricing and convenience. For several years, its ads featured a Dell and a Compaq Computer Corp. machine with technical specifications showing them to be virtually identical and price tags showing the lower cost of the Dell model. Dell's ability to beat Compaq's prices was based on its then very unusual business processes. Traditional processes related to retail stores, warehouses, and finished-goods inventory became liabilities. Faced with Dell's new system of retailing processes, some store-centered companies—Computerland, for example—went out of business.

Dell used its process edge to go from a start-up to an established firm with $3 billion in sales in a decade. Its ordering, assembly, and delivery processes became and remain its chief assets and identifying characteristics. In 1992, Dell's stock rose to $25 per share, matching the price to which Compaq's had fallen.

By 1994, however, Compaq's stock had risen to more than $100 per share and Dell's was just $27 per share. Dell had neglected forecasting and product development and had concentrated on its successful distribution processes. Forecasting was seen as a way of keeping up with short-term demand, and product development was limited to adopting Intel's new chips so that Dell could offer products that matched mainstream IBM and clone machines. When the personal computer market became more volatile, Dell's forecasting weakness and lack of innovative products became clear liabilities. In addition, competitors had entered Dell's stronghold of mail-order selling.

Dell's problems were compounded by investors' perception of its financial management processes. Dell's investor-relations processes were not just negligent; they were destructive. In 1993, when investment firm analysts complained about Dell's issuing inaccurate and incomplete financial information and failing to keep them informed about earning trends, founder Michael Dell told them in an acrimonious meeting that he didn't care what they thought: he still ran the most successful computer company in the world. Because of inaccurate financial information—and perhaps also the acrimony—Dell's stock price dropped substantially.

In the meantime, Compaq had faced up to its own crises (precipitated in part by Dell). When it became clear that the firm had been drifting toward mediocrity, its founder was fired, and the new leadership invested heavily in processes related to capital, commitment, and organization. The company overhauled the product development processes that had always been the basis of its identity and success (Compaq had been the first company to manufacture a portable computer with all the capabilities of a desktop IBM machine) and retooled its distribution processes, moving from reliance on resellers who sold to large corporations in bulk to mass merchandising and to contracting directly with companies for large-volume sales and technical support. It raised the priority of processes, such as procurement and pricing, that it had considered relatively unimportant. It invested heavily in new production processes. By mid-1995, Compaq was a different company from the one it had been in 1992. It offered a stream of innovative products and became a price leader.

Compaq and Dell had reversed their relative positions in just three years. It was Dell's turn to revamp its processes in response to Compaq's process improvements. Both firms had become successful through process but relied too long on their most successful processes, neglecting others that became important as conditions changed. They regained their leadership positions only when they renewed their attention to process improvement. By mid-1995, Dell was the seventh largest computer company in the world. Its sales had grown to more than $3 billion per year, and its stock price was $45 per share after having fallen to $13 per share in 1993. It had drastically improved its product development, cost control, and financial management and in 1994 it provided the largest investor return of any Fortune 500 company. In a competitive industry in which so many companies have gone under, both Dell and Compaq look like survivors. The process crisis was over.[1]

Applying Dell's and Compaq's processes to the salience/worth matrix shows how processes affected the companies' relative success over time. In 1992, when Dell's stock rose and Compaq's fell to the same $25 figure, convenient mail ordering and UPS delivery were what set Dell apart, what customers thought of when they thought of Dell; these are clearly identity processes. Pricing, although not equally a part of Dell's basic identity, was key to its success vis-à-vis Compaq. A failure in this process (that is, any price disadvantage) would have had a significant and immediate effect on the company. These identity and priority processes were assets because they were the main sources of company value. Forecasting, product development, and investor relations were liabilities: they were viewed as adding no value to the company. In the business environment of 1992, however, this was not a major problem for a firm with so strong an identity. Although it costs the company money, a background liability does not drain value in the way that an identity or priority liability would (see Figure 2-2A).

FIGURE 2-2A

THE SALIENCE/WORTH MATRIX FOR DELL COMPUTER, 1992

SALIENCE	WORTH	
	ASSETS	LIABILITIES
Identity	Ordering, delivery	
Priority	Pricing	
Background		Forecasting, product development, investor relations
Mandated		

In 1992, Compaq's procurement, distribution, and pricing—which had been background liabilities and therefore not absolutely critical to the company's success—were turned into priority liabilities when Dell made these its own identity and priority processes. A small potential disadvantage had become a large, actual one. At the same time, Compaq's principal identity and priority processes—product development and manufacturing—were in danger of becoming liabilities, because the company had not been paying sufficient attention to them. When identity and priority processes are liabilities or threaten to become so, decline or failure follow. The Compaq matrix is a picture of a company in trouble, a fact borne out by Compaq's falling stock price (see Figure 2-2B).

After Compaq's new management faced up to its problems in 1993 and initiated process reform that ranged from product development to distribution to pricing, product development and manufacturing were again strong assets. Procurement, distribution, and pricing went from background to priority processes to meet the challenges from Dell and other competitors (see Figure 2-3A). These changes at Compaq and throughout the computer industry affected the Dell matrix. Forecasting, product development, and investor relations, always liabilities but relatively harmless

FIGURE 2-2B

THE SALIENCE/WORTH MATRIX FOR COMPAQ, 1992

SALIENCE	WORTH	
	ASSETS	LIABILITIES
Identity	Product development ⟶	
Priority	Manufacturing ⟶	
Background		Procurement, distribution, pricing
Mandated		

background ones in 1992, became priority liabilities in 1993 (see Figure 2-3B). With its weak product development processes, Dell had no new products comparable to the laptops that Compaq was producing in 1993, and the value of Dell's stock fell. Those processes had to become a priority if Dell was to be successful again. When Dell did improve these processes, its stock rebounded from a low of $13 in 1993 to $45 in 1995.

The seesaw history of Dell and Compaq shows how important processes are to a firm's success and also suggests how readily the salience or worth can change. There is no ultimate answer to the question of which processes matter most and whether a given process adds value to a company or drains it. The salience of distribution and pricing went from background to priority for Compaq and other computer companies because Dell changed the terms of competition. The salience of product development went from background to priority for Dell because of the speed of technological improvement. Some of Compaq's asset priorities threatened to become liabilities because of neglect. Both the environment within a company and the larger environment in which it competes are dynamic, not static, and process value requires continuing attention.

Some changes in the location of processes on a company's salience/worth matrix are unintended and others deliberate. The decline of a process from an asset to a liability is clearly unintended, whether the cause is neglect within the company, a change

FIGURE 2-3A

THE SALIENCE/WORTH MATRIX FOR COMPAQ, 1993

SALIENCE	WORTH	
	ASSETS	LIABILITIES
Identity	Product development	
Priority	Manufacturing, procurement, distribution, pricing	
Background		
Mandated		

FIGURE 2-3B

THE SALIENCE/WORTH MATRIX FOR DELL, 1993

SALIENCE	WORTH	
	ASSETS	LIABILITIES
Identity	Ordering, delivery	
Priority	Pricing	Forecasting, product development, investor relations
Background		
Mandated		

in the business environment, or both. The merchandising and store management processes at Sears and Kmart, which were major assets to these firms in the 1970s, became liabilities in the 1980s, when Wal-Mart, Circuit City, and other discount stores developed replenishment processes that led to greater customer value than the older chains could offer. Similarly, Computerland's retailing processes, once assets, were turned into liabilities by Dell's ordering and delivery system. The shift in Dell's product development process from background liability to priority liability was also clearly unintended, the result of industry changes. In all of these examples, obviously, the companies concerned had no intention of making their processes less valuable. In fact, they were generally unaware of what was happening until their businesses began to decline.

Deliberate changes in process salience and worth are made either reactively, in response to business environment changes, or proactively, to gain an advantage over the competition. Compaq's determination to turn its liability pricing and distribution processes into assets was reactive, a response to Dell, just as Dell's working to make its product development process a priority asset was a response to the competitive pressure created by Compaq and other personal computer manufacturers. Dell's initial decision to focus on efficient mail ordering and common-carrier delivery was proactive, the development of new identity processes that changed the rules of competition and forced the rest of the industry to react.

MCI Communications Corp., second to AT&T in long-distance telecommunications, provides another example of the proactive development of a new identity process to gain a competitive advantage. In the late 1980s, MCI turned necessary "minor" processes—accounting and billing—into the immensely successful "Friends and Family" service that provides discounts for phone calls between members of a specified group. These processes had been background liabilities—necessary administrative processes that absorbed significant capital without providing significant returns. MCI deliberately and creatively transformed background accounting processes into an identity process that was also a product (see Figure 2-4).

Friends and Family was a considerable success. Although many commentators expressed doubt that MCI could win the 12 to 15 percent market share it was thought to need to survive against AT&T, MCI captured more than 20 percent of that market. That Friends and Family is an identity asset was reinforced by AT&T ads that tried to belittle the value of the service. When British Telecom acquired 20 percent of MCI in the 1990s, it re-created Friends and Family domestically and met with a similar positive response from consumers.

FIGURE 2-4

MCI: BACKGROUND LIABILITY BECOMES IDENTITY ASSET

SALIENCE	WORTH	
	ASSETS	LIABILITIES
Identity	"Friends and Family" service	
Priority		
Background		Accounting and billing processes
Mandated		

PROCESS PREDATORS

Dell and MCI both explicitly used business processes to create and sustain value at the expense of firms that relied on traditional processes without realizing that their value is being eroded by other companies' innovations. I call such opportunistic, innovative companies "process predators." Predators use business processes to change the rules of competition. Often they take background liability processes such as ordering, delivery, and billing and turn them into identity asset processes that become major competitive advantages and sources of value.

Federal Express was a process predator whose guarantee of overnight delivery (its identity process), supported by its invention of airline hubbing, changed the rules of small-package delivery. Its new way of doing business turned the processes of the postal service and the airlines that had controlled package delivery into liabilities. *USA Today* developed the first successful national newspaper in the United States thanks to new communications and information management processes. Storing news items, editorial material, and graphics electronically and using satellite transmission to send them across the country and to Europe for use in locally printed editions, *USA Today* solved the problem of producing a nationwide (and international) newspaper with timely, relevant news in all its editions. Production processes, rather than the quality of reporting or editing, are at the heart of the company's success. When the *New York Times* had earlier tried to publish a West Coast edition, its lack of process capabilities meant that it could only produce a California version of a New York publication, and the venture failed.

The word *predator* suggests a sudden, overwhelming attack, but process predators rarely capture the markets they enter without long effort and considerable uncertainty. Now that Federal Express is a household name, it is easy to forget that the firm's early years were troubled, with bankruptcy seeming more probable than survival. It took more than a decade for *USA Today* to reach the break-even point. No firm can create a sustainable asset instantly: it takes time to develop and perfect an identity process and the other processes needed to support it. Reengineering, total quality management, and other process movements provide no quick fix. Processes should be thought of as capital; the return on process investment is not immediate but comes over time, like the return on other capital investments.

THE PRIMACY OF IDENTITY PROCESSES

Identity processes have a special importance for firms. The processes for which a firm is known must remain its principal source of value if it is going to thrive. The successful process predators I have described all have strong identity process assets that give them an edge; a company with identity process liabilities is bound to be in serious trouble. If Federal Express was no longer able to guarantee on-time package delivery, it would cease to be a viable company. Even a temporary decline in reliability would damage its reputation and give competitors an opportunity to take away its business. The most dramatic stories of corporate success and corporate decline have to do with identity processes.

McDONALD'S: IDENTITY PROCESS PAYOFF

The success of McDonald's Corp. derives from the company's maintenance of identity process assets. It sells a product that is difficult to differentiate: with minor variations, hamburger is hamburger, and anyone can make French fries. The advantage for McDonald's is its identity as a consistent and reliable provider of quality food at a competitive price. Many of its processes focus on supporting this reputation. The company has established clear and unvarying timing and sequencing for fast-food preparation. Its training is based on the idea of standardized processes executed flawlessly. Its cultural norms emphasize reliability and consistency. Even with close to 100 percent annual staff turnover, its efficiency is high.

McDonald's is a processes-driven firm. Processes that other firms would think of as background—for instance, training—are prioritized by management. Because they are seen as essential to maintaining the McDonald's identity, they get the attention and investment they need. Management bases company priorities and strategies so thoroughly on its business processes that it is not unreasonable to say that processes are the secular religion of McDonald's. When the entrepreneur who owns 80 percent of a McDonald's restaurant buys a McDonald's franchise, he or she is mainly buying a coordinated set of processes that cover virtually every element of operations.

Firms that tried to imitate McDonald's have failed: lacking its total commitment to process, they found that building process assets required huge investments of capital, which is far costlier and takes more time than buying restaurants and copying menus. There is no secret ingredient in the hamburgers that gives McDonald's an edge. The company's success comes from the fact that its investment, experience, culture, and management all support the processes that create its identity. That unified process focus is what competitors find difficult to match.

IBM: IDENTITY PROCESS PROBLEMS

For decades, marketing and cultural processes were IBM's identity assets, defining what the company stood for and how customers and investors saw it. The close relationship between IBM's sales force and corporate clients was the firm's hallmark. It was not just hardware and software being sold but a partnership and a point of view. IBM's identity processes reflected and were supported by control, incentive, training, and promotion processes that created an ideology: shared attitudes and behaviors added up to "the IBM way" (this in fact was the title of a best-seller in 1980s). The company's slowness, administrative complexity, and overhead were notorious, but these were background liabilities. Customers accepted them as a necessary nuisance, offset by the fact that IBM provided unique and essential value. A salience/worth matrix of some of these key processes in the 1970s is shown in Figure 2-5.

By the late 1980s, however, dramatic developments in the computer industry had seriously eroded IBM's position. Like other market leaders, the company was slow to recognize changes that threatened the basis of its success. The marketing and cultural processes that had been assets in selling and supporting complex, costly mainframe systems became liabilities in an environment in which small, powerful, less expensive computers and open systems could perform many of the same functions. The processes that IBM built and maintained at immense cost and that customers had once trusted and valued had turned into identity liabilities, draining value instead of adding it. At the same time, the background liabilities that had been an acceptable inefficiency when the company dominated the world market became identity liabilities: slowness, financial waste, and bureaucratic complexity were now what the company was known for (see Figure 2-6). When IBM's stock price fell, the company initiated a severe round of layoffs for the first time in its history, and new management was brought in to try to find a new direction for the firm. The lesson is clear: identity process liabilities spell disaster.

A TOOL FOR DECISION-MAKING

In applying some well-known business cases to the salience/worth matrix, I have used it to analyze how and why certain processes have affected the success of these companies. At the same time, the examples demonstrate the critical importance of processes to firms—especially their identity and priority processes. They also give a sense of the many factors that can change the

FIGURE 2-5

THE SALIENCE/WORTH MATRIX FOR IBM, 1970s

SALIENCE	WORTH	
	ASSETS	LIABILITIES
Identity	Marketing Cultural processes	
Priority		
Background		Complex administrative processes and bureaucratic culture
Mandated		

FIGURE 2-6

THE SALIENCE/WORTH MATRIX FOR IBM, LATE 1980s

SALIENCE	WORTH	
	ASSETS	LIABILITIES
Identity		Marketing Cultural processes Complex administrative processes and bureaucratic culture
Priority		
Background		
Mandated		

salience and worth of processes in a way that affects the firm's success or survival.

The primary purpose of the salience/worth matrix, however, is to give managers a tool for understanding their companies' processes—an understanding that will enable them to make informed decisions about which processes to invest in and what kind of investments should be made. The next two chapters focus on how to determine the salience and worth of processes in an organization.

CHAPTER 3

OUT OF
THE PROCESS
SWAMP

DETERMINING SALIENCE

NAMING ALL THE PROCESSES THAT GO ON WITHIN A FIRM IS NOT a simple task: the sheer number is daunting. Business processes are much more numerous than many analysts realize.

THE PROCESS SWAMP

Thomas Davenport, a thoughtful commentator on business processes, argues that "most companies, even large and complex ones, can be broken down into fewer than twenty major processes." He says that IBM has eighteen major processes; Xerox Corp., fourteen; and Dow Chemical, nine.[1] Michael Hammer and James Champy bluntly assert that "hardly any company contains more than ten or so principal processes."[2]

The number you arrive at obviously depends on your definition of *major* or *principal*. Andersen Consulting has published a database that identifies 170 important business processes.[3] Daven-port doesn't list the 18 IBM processes he considers major, but I can immediately name 60 that might merit the term. In fact, I can list 300 IBM processes that have annual budgets of more than $200 million (one reasonable definition of *major*), and I can quickly add another 50 cultural and management processes that cost less but have a significant effect on the company. I define "major business process" as one that has or might have an important impact on a firm's value and concomitant success. Figure 3-1 shows about 100 common processes to which this definition applies.

Many of these are top-level processes that can be broken down into subprocesses. Research and development, for instance, includes project selection, research funding, engineering design, and other procedures. Companies have thousands of processes, not "ten or so," and for obvious reasons I call the immensity of these processes the "process swamp"—a complex, dynamic, and seemingly formless assortment of processes, some closely con-nected to others, others related only slightly or not at all. There are few or no obvious guides as to which ones are important or how changes in one may affect the others. Managers trying to identify key processes or to understand the relative importance of, say, hiring processes versus investment processes versus distribution processes may well feel that they are drowning in a multitude of choices.

Many managers simply don't know what really makes their companies work. When the executives of Digital Equipment Corp. (DEC), for several decades the leader in the non-IBM computer industry, met to discuss why a massive reorganization left the com-pany still ineffective and inefficient, they uncovered a problem that exists in many firms:

> At the end of the three-hour meeting, Ken Olsen [DEC's founder] sat back in his chair with a stunned look on his face. . . . "What you're telling me is the senior managers in this company that are making commitments to me have no idea how this company oper-ates?" "On an operational level," [the executive responsible for business process redesign] remembers responding, "that's exactly what I'm telling you." . . . [I]t's no different at most companies.

FIGURE 3-1

THE PROCESS SWAMP

customer service   inventory management   shipping
warehousing   investment planning   acquisition
channel management   team rewards   security
public relations   regulatory compliance   safety   communication
hiring   supplier relations   training   decision making   budgeting   R&D   legal
production planning   organizational design   downsizing planning
product launch   promotion   risk management   payments branding
risk management   quality control   forecasting   governance   shareholder relations
manufacturing   credit control   performance evaluation   corporate governance   tax
lobbying   personnel records   medical   freight
management development   records management   sales support   warranty claims
travel management   insurance   office management   outsourcing alliance
divestment   information systems planning   project management   competitive assessment
executive compensation   purchasing   cash management   invoicing   product launch
pricing   customer retention   marketing   change management   cost control
salary policy   benefits management   loans   technology assessment
financial control   global financing   benchmarking   innovation
executive compensation   capital investment   pension administration
negotiation   engineering   market research   accounting
management succession
catering   account management
environmental
data center
learning

That is, senior managers just don't know how their company conducts its business operations. [The executive added], "Real operational performance is no longer understood."[4]

Some movements try to solve the process swamp problem by deciding that there is no swamp. As I have mentioned, a definition that limits processes to work flows will ignore a great many processes and produce a simpler (but dangerously incomplete) picture. Total quality management typically zeroes in on manufacturing, manufacturing-related processes, or those processes (safety, for example) that lend themselves to precise, objective quality measurement. Total quality management is likely to identify and focus on the relatively small group of processes shown in Figure 3-2.

FIGURE 3-2

THE TYPICAL TQM NAVIGATION
THROUGH THE PROCESS SWAMP

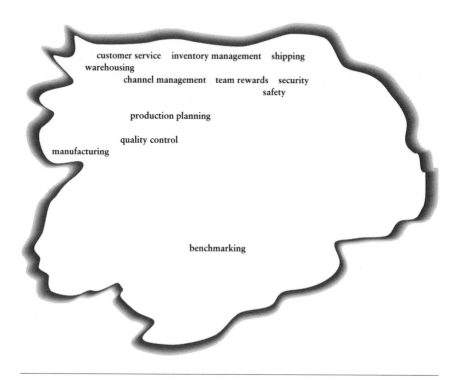

customer service   inventory management   shipping
warehousing
channel management   team rewards   security
safety

production planning

quality control

manufacturing

benchmarking

Similarly, reengineering will often address customer service, logistics, or product development but will probably ignore hiring and management succession. If it does pay any attention to them, it will concern itself with subsets of the processes whose work flows match the tools that reengineering experts know how to use. A reengineering perspective may see the swamp the way it is depicted in Figure 3-3.

NAVIGATING THE SWAMP

These simplifications are superficially attractive. They seem to solve the problem of the swamp by concentrating on a set of

FIGURE 3-3

THE TYPICAL INDUSTRIAL ENGINEERING/ REENGINEERING NAVIGATION

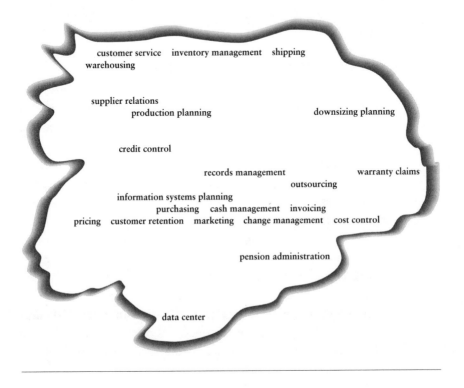

processes small enough to be analyzed and managed. These processes may not be the ones that really matter, however. When selection is based on a limited definition of what a process is or on the match between a process and the availability of familiar tools to improve it, the company runs the risk of investing in the wrong processes. This creates the process paradox, of course: measurable process improvement accompanied by measurable corporate decline. Neither TQM nor reengineering would be likely to address acquisition, financial investment, or public relations processes, but these may be the very ones that offer a firm the greatest process payoff. To avoid the process paradox and to navigate the process swamp, we need a systematic method of evaluating processes that does not a priori exclude any types of processes and does not assume that the same processes will have equal value in every company and situation. It should be clear by now that the salience/worth matrix meets those requirements. Defining processes according to their salience and worth clarifies their true value to the company. Once processes are understood in terms of those qualities, process investment decisions can be approached with confidence.

This chapter focuses on salience. Determining the salience of a given business process involves sequential elimination: If the process is not an identity one, is it priority? If not priority, is it background? If not background, is it mandated? If it is none of these, it must be a folklore process. The essential questions to ask at each elimination point are listed in Figure 3-4.

This analytical process goes a long way toward helping managers get their bearings in the process swamp. It can be applied to any business process, and the resulting classification immediately begins to suggest the kind of attention that the process is likely to require. Processes defined as *identity* or *priority* will obviously warrant a closer look than folklore processes. Examining a range of organizational processes using this tool creates a clear picture of those that really matter to a firm. Determining salience accurately is not as simple as the clear decisions in Figure 3-4 may suggest, however. Although the questions asked at each stage are basic, their answers are not necessarily self-evident. Federal Express obviously knows that on-time delivery is an identity process; McDonald's does not need to be told that consistency is part of its identity. Those firms have succeeded by understanding which processes define them and which are critically important to their performance. Not every firm has that kind of insight (or that kind of success). In my work with companies on process investment, I have found a range of management process knowledge that goes from blindness to awareness to understanding to insight. Firms that are blind to the importance of many of their own processes or are merely aware of the fact that processes matter will have difficulty answering the key questions correctly. Let's look at some of the common errors that prevent managers from making an accurate determination of process salience.

FIGURE 3-4

EVALUATING THE PROCESS PORTFOLIO

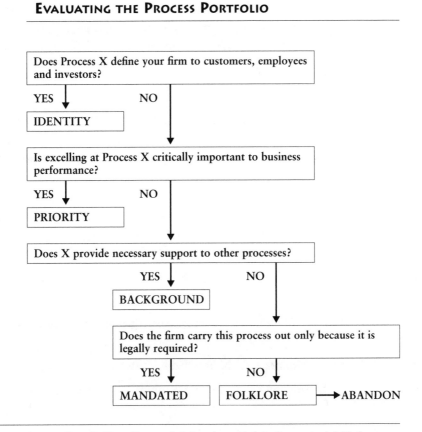

SOURCE: Dorothy Yu at Coopers & Lybrand provided the first version of this figure.

DISCOUNTING

Discounting means ignoring or underestimating the importance of a business process. Historically, most managers have felt little need to pay attention to processes. They have been concerned with inputs to processes and outputs from them, but they downgrade or discount the importance of the processes themselves. Take, for example, the back-office processes in financial services firms. Even the words *back office* suggest that these processes are viewed as background activity, not as important to the firm as other activities or especially worthy of managerial attention. Trading and selling are usually considered the glamour jobs in the securities industry, and deal-makers tend to get the most attention and biggest promotions in corporate banking. The back office has been dismissed as "overhead" or "administration." In most insurance companies, back-office claims processing is given lower priority than underwriting and brokering. Back-office employees are generally less skilled and receive lower pay than underwriters and brokers. But the claims department is the one department with which customers have direct contact. For customers, back-office processes are very much in the foreground. They do not interact with underwriters; their broker is the intermediary they deal with when they buy their policy.

As a result of being discounted, back-office functions have often been underfunded and undermanaged. These are the characteristics that managers typically think such processes should exhibit:

- stability of process and of the units that carry it out
- low turnover, with limited need for ongoing training
- division of labor, with process steps split into well-defined substeps that are often handled by different departments
- an orientation to financial inputs and outputs, performance objects, staffing levels, direct and allocated costs, and business justification in terms of results

Managers of such processes are rewarded for staying within budget and meeting output quotas. If they do so, their superiors are unlikely to question the process or look closely at how it is carried out. As long as a process works, they are content to leave it alone.

This is not necessarily a bad thing. By looking only at budgets and performance, managers effectively delegate the process to a subordinate, thus reducing their own coordination and communication costs, freeing up time and energy to devote to more pressing matters, and empowering the process manager to carry out that role as he or she sees fit. Although many in the process movement have cited this hierarchical and bureaucratic way of managing as a problem and have even blamed it for the weakness of U.S. business, there is in fact nothing fundamentally wrong with it. In the appropriate situation, it may be the way to get the most economic value out of a process. Sometimes leaving a process alone is the best thing to do with it. And sometimes a process that runs "like a machine" is the right one for accomplishing a mechanical task.

Discounting can, however, obstruct the determination of salience. Stability can become ossification of process and staff; personnel can become obsessed with following established rules, even when the reasons for doing so cease to be valid; and promotion may rest on going along to get along, rather than on competence and initiative. Judged only on the basis of budgets and performance, staff may find ways to bypass or distort these measures. Above all, changing business conditions can turn a once-successful process into a liability. If the internal problems just described can be avoided, a stable process that works well will continue to work well in a stable environment. It is clear, though, that to all managers change is now the rule, and reliance on the status quo is a recipe for either mediocrity or failure. Wang, DEC, and IBM are only three companies that suffered financially by ignoring a changing business environment or by assuming that the changes would not affect them—that the processes that succeeded in the past would be successful in the future.

By discounting processes that have traditionally been considered of secondary importance or have always "taken care of themselves," managers may underestimate the value of many corporate processes and their role in the firm's success. Or they may miss an opportunity to create economic value that could be realized by intentionally raising the salience of a background process. (This was the strategy for MCI's "Friends and Family" service that I discussed in Chapter 2 and will discuss extensively later.) Whatever the case, discounting means failing to evaluate a process with an open mind and believing that the process's value is already known.

REIFICATION

Process movements that think only in terms of work flows are guilty of reification, or turning processes into *things*. They define processes as distinct sets of visible actions with measurable inputs and outputs: sequential building blocks that lead to some clear end product. The only business activities they regard as processes are the ones that fit this definition; decision-making, establishing or modifying cultural norms, or employee relations do not appear on their process maps, even though they may be of more consequence to the firm than work flows.

Managers with insight solely into work-flow processes are blind to other key processes. Whereas discounting causes managers to assign the wrong salience to some processes, reification results in processes being ignored altogether. The dangers inherent in this incomplete process analysis should be clear by now. Remember that both General Motors and IBM received the Baldrige Award for the quality of their work flows at the same time that flaws in other processes were leading these companies into crisis. Customers saw benefits from the processes that created General Motors' new line of Saturn cars, but the company continued to lose value everywhere, mainly through a range of faulty decision-making processes. General Motors continued its long-standing tradition of internal sourcing when other automakers had turned to more flexible and economical outsourcing. Its product development processes led to an uncoordinated product line, with competing models and major gaps. (Coordination is a process concept.) The power of its central financial staff created a wasteful bureaucracy and led to senior management's receiving misleading information about the firm's economic health. Labor relations processes brought cost, conflict, and loss of trust. One chairman's acquisition and technology investment processes resulted in his spending approximately $54 billion on failed ventures; he could have bought the entire Japanese car industry at the time for $35 billion. Reification ignores all of these process problems while focusing on work-flow improvements.

Reification also tends to result in blindness to process economics. The work-flow view of processes does not offer a sound economic model. It does not help managers decide which of the many processes that affect long-term value for customer and company should be invested in; it does not adequately measure the benefits of process improvement against the true costs.

TRADITIONAL THINKING: THE MYTH OF INDUSTRY CORE PROCESSES

The most widespread cause of process blindness is looking at business processes within the context of a traditional industry. This kind of bounded thinking takes an industry as the unit of strategic analysis, as if industries were unchanging, readily definable entities. This attitude considers only the processes, products, and services that have been traditionally associated with one or another industry. Over the last two decades, however, deregulation and technology, among other factors, have blurred the traditional distinctions between industries and have changed the rules of competition. Consider the following firms in the context of their supposed "industry."

- **BRITISH AIRWAYS.** An airline that is a major player in the hotel reservations business. Because passengers and travel agents book flights before they book hotel rooms, the company is in a position to capture the customer at the key moment and pre-empt the hotel industry itself. British Airways has significant control of the hotel industry's product and pricing. Hotels must pay a steep commission to the airline or risk losing business to the hotels that deal with British Airways.

- **AT&T.** Struggling in its "core" business of telecommunications and a major player in credit cards.

- **USAA.** An insurer that is among America's top five issuers of mutual funds and car loans.

- **McKESSON.** A leading pharmacy supplier company but also— using its electronic data handling capabilities—the fourth largest processor of health care insurance industry claims in the United States.

- **GENERAL MOTORS** and **FORD.** Automakers that are also the nation's largest holders of consumer credit, each with more than $100 billion in financial assets. Like British Airways providing timely hotel reservations services, these firms capitalize on the fact that they are on the spot when the customer needs financing. GM's credit subsidiary has often made more money in a given year than its manufacturing operations.

Each of these firms has extended its mainstream processes beyond its industry's traditional boundaries and into the domain of another industry, thereby creating a new business area for the company.

The theory that industry drives competitive positioning, explicated skillfully and influentially by Michael Porter in *Competitive Strategy*, suggests that processes are industry-specific and that each industry can identify a set of core processes that its firms have in common. Obviously, firms that sell the same products and services must use many of the same processes. But, as my examples make clear, processes that supposedly "belong" to one industry can be used to advantage in another, and processes that may or may not be at the core of one aspect of a company's business can be at the core of another. British Airways' reservations processes are part of both its airline business and its hotel reservations business. General Motors' consumer credit processes are not among the core processes of automobile manufacturing, but they are at the heart of the company's financing business.

Traditional thinking fails to consider the salience of processes that are not central to traditional industry activities but may be important to the firm or integral to new business opportunities and sources of value.

SALIENCE VARIABILITY

It is clear from much of what I have said that the salience of a given process is not necessarily the same in different companies and different circumstances. This is even true within industries. Virtually all insurance firms have underwriting, customer contact, and claims processes, but different firms give those processes markedly different salience. UNUM, a leading disability insurance company, prides itself on underwriting. It claims that its underwriters can distinguish between the actuarial risks of two doctors, one left-handed and one right-handed, who drive identical Volvos and live in New Jersey, and can set policy prices accordingly. UNUM's underwriting and pricing are identity processes. The company's clients, however, may never have heard of UNUM, because it works mainly through brokers; branding and customer contact are very much background processes. The State Farm Group, by contrast, invests heavily in brand recognition and gets value from being perhaps the best-known name in the industry.

USAA's reputation and success rest on the superb customer contact services that are its identity processes. For decades, its business goal has been to make dealing with USAA easier than having an insurance agent next door. A single phone call links customers to a service agent who has access to every piece of information about policies, payments, customer history, and anything else that may be needed to answer questions or handle a transaction. An agent can issue a policy or a automobile loan in as little as six minutes. USAA is the world's largest user of 800 numbers.

Progressive insurance is a leader in on-the-spot claims processing for automobile accidents. Its claims adjusters work from vans equipped with mobile communications devices, computers, and printers. They drive around their territories and can often arrive at an accident scene within minutes, processing the claim and issuing a check on the spot. Because the company specializes in high-risk drivers, some of whom have made fraudulent claims in this past, this rapid response system limits opportunities for fraud and keeps costs down. Claims processing, relegated to the back office in many firms, is an identity process for Progressive.

So one kind of salience variability is the different valuation that firms (even those in the same business) place on the same basic process. The salience of a process is not necessarily fixed either: it can be changed by alterations in the business environment (as competition from small, powerful computers and open systems raised IBM's administrative processes from background to identity), and it can be changed intentionally within a company (as MCI raised its accounting and billing processes from background to identity process with its "Friends and Family" service).

Furthermore, the salience of a process is likely to be judged differently by different groups of people within organizations. In a professional services firm, for instance, the staff is likely to consider time-sheet reporting a background liability. They may think of it as a bureaucratic chore that takes time away from their priority-asset processes of marketing and client project work, which directly generate value for the firm. The company's senior partners, though, may consider time-sheet reporting a priority process that tracks cash flow, productivity, working capital, and the efficiency and timeliness of billing. Similarly, a hospital physician will probably consider insurance claims processing a background liability that wastes valuable time and erodes his or her ability to provide the best and promptest care for patients. For the hospital manager, however, it will undoubtedly be a priority (although possibly a liability, in that it may drain value). The same physician may see patient scheduling as a priority-asset process that increases efficiency and fees, ensuring no "dead time" when there's no next patient in line. The patient, of course, will probably judge the same scheduling process a background liability, as his or her time is being treated as less valuable than the physician's.

THE MANAGER'S TASK

Analyzing the salience of a firm's processes is an important task that requires considerable thought and insight, even under the guidance of the salience/worth matrix. As we have seen, one of several complexities to be considered is that different groups and individuals see the salience of the same process differently. So the question "Whose valuation counts most?" must be answered before a process's importance to the entire firm can be determined.

WHOSE VALUATION?

Most process movements stress the importance of looking at processes from the customer's point of view. Customer service and satisfaction are explicit goals of many of these movements, including reengineering and TQM. Most standard definitions of business processes are framed in terms of the customer. As Hammer and Champy write, "We define a business process as a collection of activities that takes one or more kinds of input and creates an output that is of value to the customer."[5] This customer focus has limitations, however. For one thing, it overlooks mandated processes such as tax reporting and may ignore some background processes whose connection with customer value seems especially tenuous.

Also, it does not sufficiently consider the cost of customer satisfaction. After all, if the only objective were to ensure complete customer satisfaction, firms would give their products away.

In the long run, it is investors' valuation of a process that counts most. Investors, in this context, include not only stockholders but financial experts and investment houses that set the market price of a firm's stock and the agencies that fund a public-sector organization's budgets. In determining salience and seeking out process investment opportunities, managers need to ask how investors would value the process, or rather, how they would recognize and assess the value of improving it. Investors are more likely to see the impact of a process than its details. If investors do not perceive that an improved process will create EVA, they will not bid up the company's stock price or fund the budget. Nor, ultimately, will they continue to buy the company's products and services. Customers are investors, too, although not the only ones. Neither Mutual Benefit's investors—the people who had their funds in the company—nor New Jersey state regulators saw the economic value of the company's brilliant reengineering of policy-issuing processes. What they saw were Mutual Benefit's much more critical liabilities. The questions as to whether a process defines the company to investors (as well as to customers and employees) and whether it is critical to business performance help clarify the link between process and investor value.

Managers need to ensure that there is no serious contradiction between the salience valuations of investors, internal managers, and staff. The manager who comes to understand the value of the firm's processes from the investor's viewpoint must educate his or her coworkers about their importance. Managers unwilling to invest in key processes and staff who only grudgingly carry out essential processes that they consider pointless or irritating put a firm's current and future economic health at risk.

MAKING SENSE OF THE PROCESS SWAMP

I can provide no reliable answer to the question of how many major business processes a firm has. Nor can I provide a generic list of important processes. Business processes do not sort themselves into a tidy inventory. Total quality management and reengineering attempt to make process evaluation manageable by looking at only a few processes. The salience/worth matrix does not exclude any class of business processes. I think of it as a broad funnel that managers should fill by being open-minded and imaginative in their consideration of processes. While asking themselves (and one another) which processes identify the firm, which are critically important, which provide necessary support, and so forth, they should also consider how business environment changes are likely to affect their processes. They should look carefully at processes that are prone to being devalued by discounting: the administrative, back-office processes that may be more valuable than they at first assume. They should consider processes that reification might cause them to ignore: non–work-flow processes related to hiring, training, promotion, communications, and decision-making. They should try to free themselves from the traditional thinking that already "knows" which processes matter and which are insignificant in their industry. They should ask themselves, "If we were taking over this firm, which processes would we pay most attention to because they seemed to provide opportunities to generate and sustain value?"

This kind of openness and imagination, and the inclusiveness of the salience/worth matrix (inclusive in that it doesn't exclude any type of process, unlike the work flow conception), will initially generate a longer list of processes than can be considered in depth. A process investment initiative that had to keep hundreds or even thousands of processes in view for any length of time would never get anywhere. But by considering the *worth* of processes—asking which are assets and which liabilities—managers can quickly pare down the initial list and will likely be left with only the ten to twenty processes that matter most. These processes—the ones investors care about—are all the major processes that a company can and must pay attention to. They constitute the firm's process investment portfolio.

CHAPTER 4

PROCESS WORTH AND EVA

THE BASIC PRINCIPLE OF PROCESS WORTH IS SIMPLE: ANY process that returns more money than it costs adds value to the firm and is therefore an asset; a process that costs more than it returns drains value and is therefore a liability. A process that does not tie up substantial capital is value-neutral. The procedures for determining process worth and locating processes in the asset or liability column of the salience/worth matrix (while eliminating value-neutral processes from consideration) are diagrammed in Figure 4-1.

To determine a business process's worth to their firms, managers have to answer two questions:

- Approximately how much capital does the firm have tied up in the process?

- Does the process generate a positive cash flow after the cost of the capital has been deducted?

FIGURE 4-1

DETERMINING PROCESS WORTH

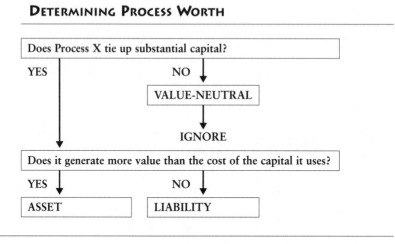

If the answer to the first question is "Not much," then the process is value-neutral and need not be considered further. The cost of capital invested in a process includes direct and indirect capital investments as well as direct expenses and hidden expenses— the often ignored process costs that are either allocated to a department or handled as corporate overhead. Notice, too, that I define the value of a process in economic terms, as positive cash flow. Qualitative "soft" process benefits such as "better" planning, "quality," or "improved" customer service may or may not generate economic value. They do not in themselves define a process as a corporate asset.[1]

Although a process's cost and generated value are basic economic considerations, I suspect that many managers will be unable to supply this data. In most instances, it is almost impossible to collect reliable information about the capital spent on existing processes. Conventional accounting systems distort and obscure capital investment by focusing on expenses. It is equally difficult to forecast the impact on a firm's cash flow of process improvements such as better customer service, reduced time to market, or the establishment of teams as the organization's basic units.

Readers might question the value of an investment framework based on costs that are nearly impossible to track and benefits that cannot be reliably related to economic return. I can reassure these skeptics, though. First of all, the simple distinction between asset and liability processes requires only an approximation of the capital invested. There is no need to collect massive data, because the underlying logic is more important than the exact numbers. As the old saying goes, it's better to be approximately correct than precisely wrong. Also, the framework's focus on the economic value a process creates (although this is not always easily determined) does identify tangible criteria for assessing genuine payoff. It substitutes firm guidelines for an often vague sense that process improvements must contribute to a company's success—an expectation disproved by the process paradox. The strongest argument for basing process investment on capital cost and economic value is that using standard accounting methods is misleading and doesn't work. Firms that rely on such indicators are likely to lose value.

DETERMINING TRUE CAPITAL COSTS: AN EXAMPLE

To see how process costs can be estimated and to get a sense of the difference between process expenses and true capital cost, let's look at a hypothetical but familiar example. Think of the department in a large firm that handles travel and entertainment accounting and reporting. Assume that it has twenty people working in it and that its annual budget is $1.2 million for salaries, allocated rent, overhead, and similar costs. Those are all expensed costs. The true cost of capital tied up in travel management, however, is the approximate total of after-tax cash paid over the past three to five years to create, operate, and maintain the process. Most of these costs will not show up in the department's budget, and many will be undocumented. For instance, use of the firm's software systems for travel management may be charged to travel, but it is unlikely that anyone in the company knows how much was spent to develop those systems (which probably include programs for analyzing travel patterns, monitoring compliance with company rules, tracking supplier discounts, and so forth). My conservative guess is that software development represents at least $20 million in capital costs, with annual maintenance, operations, and enhancements amounting to $12 million. Each of the twenty people in the department will have at least one personal computer, and there may be several special-purpose airline and hotel reservations terminals. The support cost for these systems, largely hidden in an information services budget, will be at least $10,000 per unit per year, adding another $250,000 to the cash actually invested in the department.

In addition, the visible costs of the travel department are likely to be dwarfed by the cost of time spent by business units in travel management and reporting. There are probably more full-time-equivalent staff handling travel in the business units than the twenty people in travel. Add storage and archival space, training, and other costs either directly or indirectly attributable to travel management and the capital cost of the process is probably close to $40 million, of which the department's $1.2 million budget is only a small fraction. Because the cost of capital for a large company is typically around 12 percent, that $40 million represents almost $5 million diverted from free cash flow. (*Free cash flow* is a term coined by the finance theorists whose work generated the highly pragmatic tools of EVA. It's the real money the firm has after it has calculated the taxes it must pay, paid its due loans and interest, and sent out its dividend checks. Free cash flow is the money it has added through its EVA.) Some of the money will be recovered through tax savings that result from expensing costs, but the total is still a much larger drain on value than the apparent pretax process "cost" of $1.2 million in budgeted expenses.

Estimating the "cost" of capital can be a complex exercise, but a simple rule of thumb will do: an averagely successful company can arrive at a reasonably accurate figure by adding 6 percent to its cost of borrowing; an above-average company, 3 percent; a below-average company, 9 percent. In late 1996, that meant that the average cost of capital for large firms was around 14 percent.

KINDS OF CAPITAL COSTS: A CHECKLIST

The travel department example gives us some idea of the costs that constitute the total capital investment in a process. I divide those costs into four types: direct attributable expenses, hidden expenses, direct capital investment, and indirect capital investment.

DIRECT ATTRIBUTABLE EXPENSES

Direct attributable expenses result directly from a process.[2] These are the after-tax payments (cash paid out, not amounts expensed or accrued) for salaries, benefits, materials, office supplies, and other direct expenses. A logical test of direct attributable expenses is this: if the process disappears, the cost disappears; if the level of process activity increases, direct attributable variable costs will increase. (Fixed costs, by definition, will remain the same.) Direct attributable expenses should obviously be attributed to the process, although some may not be associated with it by accounting. Accounting systems are not set up to track the end-to-end costs of a process. Hidden in many department budgets are costs directly attributable to a process but whose connection with it is not recognized. This can mislead the company about the real costs of the process and the value of the benefits it provides. An example is the cost of hiring, which companies rarely relate to processes. If they did, they might realize that finding ways to reduce turnover might be a more profitable investment than reengineering the relevant process.

Activity-based costing is a valuable tool for calculating process expenses with more accuracy than traditional accounting is likely to achieve. Developed to aid pricing, management control, and performance monitoring, activity-based costing measures the true costs of products and services by calculating apparently indirect costs such as overhead, distribution, and head office support in a new way. Traditionally, these costs have been allocated to products through a simple formula based on labor hours. This formula worked well enough when manufacturing was the dominant business and material, machinery, and labor accounted for most of a product's total cost (with everything else bundled as "overhead"). Now, however, labor accounts for less than 15 percent of product cost, even in manufacturing firms. Overhead is the largest cost component of service-dominated organizations. Allocating overhead as an indirect cost based on labor hours distorts the true cost and therefore the true profitability of products and services. Standard high-volume manufactured products that consume substantial material and labor typically are saddled with a disproportionately high fraction of marketing, engineering, finance, and head office costs. High-tech and other specialty products with low labor costs are allocated a smaller portion of these overhead costs even though they in fact may consume a larger part of the services lumped together as "overhead." As a result, these products look less expensive to make and more profitable on paper than they really are. Similarly, a firm's "best" customers—those who require substantial account team service and technical support—may actually generate less profit than those who spend less money but order large quantities of standard low-margin and low-maintenance products.

A company I worked with after it had decided to reengineer the processes by which it manufactured aluminum ladders offers an example of how activity-based costing can provide a better understanding of a product's true cost than traditional accounting. Here is the traditional accounting view of the ladder-making process before reengineering:

Selling price	$30.00
Labor, material, machinery	$12.20
Selling, distribution, administration	$6.30
Allocated overhead	$7.00
Operating profit	$4.50

Reengineering streamlined the manufacturing process, lowering the cost from $12.20 to $8.50 per ladder. This apparently increased profit to $8.20, almost double what it had been.

I say "apparently" because these figures are actually meaningless. Hidden in the $7 of allocated overhead is a portion of the cost of the corporate legal department. Because ladders account for only a small part of the company's sales, the share of legal expenditures allocated to ladder manufacture was also small. When the firm used activity-based costing to look at the end-to-end costs of the process, however, it discovered that legal expenses actually attributable to the sale of ladders were much higher than for any other product. When people fall off ladders, they tend to blame the manufacturer. Although fewer than three hundred such incidents occur each year and only a small number actually go to court, they consume many hours of the legal department's time.

An activity-based costing of the ladder-making process looks different from the traditional accounting one:

Selling Price	$30.00
Labor, material, machinery	$12.20
Selling, distribution, administration	$6.30
Legal costs	$15.00
Overhead (minus allocated legal costs)	$6.30
Operating profit	–$9.80

The company was losing almost $10 on every ladder it made. Even after a reengineering initiative that reduced manufacturing costs by 30 percent, the loss was still more than $6 for every ladder sold.

Discovering the hidden but directly attributable legal costs using the business process investment approach led the company to a simple and valuable innovation. First, it provided free accident insurance to all purchasers of ladders, at a cost to the company of $1.80 per ladder. In addition, it outsourced all legal processes to a legal services firm that absorbed the costs of compliance, litigation, and claims resolution for a fixed annual fee. The ladder maker saved $3.3 million (including the added cost of insurance), or about $11 per ladder.

Traditional accounting does not reflect this success. Savings in legal expenses are absorbed in overhead, reducing the allocation to ladders by just 40 cents. Activity-based costing led to a reduction of ladder-related legal fees from $15 to $4, making the sale of ladders profitable.

Activity-based costing is not the whole answer to estimating the capital cost of processes, as it focuses on expenses only. But by attributing expenses correctly to the activities that generate them, it can help find process costs that may be scattered across many budgets and departments.

HIDDEN EXPENSES

Hidden expenses are not directly, and sometimes not easily, attributable to a process, but they are in fact part of the cost of the process and represent some of the capital invested in it. Some common examples are

- **HUMAN RESOURCE EXPENSES** (hiring, training, and severance)

- **INFORMATION TECHNOLOGY EXPENSES** (software maintenance, support, operations, backup, and administration)

- **PROCESS OVERSIGHT EXPENSES** (management time, security, and regulatory compliance)

Hidden ongoing information technology expenses are often much higher than most managers realize. Ignoring them means that management will significantly underestimate the real cost of processes. How many companies take the following kinds of IT expenses into account when they evaluate their process costs?[3]

- **SOFTWARE DEVELOPMENT.** Every dollar spent building a software system generates, on average, 20 cents of operating expenses and 40 cents of maintenance expenses per year. (Maintenance includes updating as well as correcting errors.) So a $1 million systems development expense is really a commitment of $4 million in capital over five years.

- **SUPPORT.** According to many surveys, a $3,000 purchase of a personal computer, software, and printer costs at least $15,000 when the investment in technical support specialists, internal consultants, troubleshooters, and help desks is taken into account.

- **EDUCATION.** Educating people in how to use new systems in their work accounts for about 20 percent of the cost of a development project whose goal is to change how that work is done.

- **LOCAL AREA NETWORKS.** Additional personal computers add cost to the telecommunications systems that link the PCs. According to one detailed survey, the true cost of purchasing a $25 electronic mail package for a PC is $150 per year.

Many of these hidden costs are omitted from business analyses and justifications of investments in process improvement, making actual cost much higher than the "official" figures. On average, the immediate visible cost of IT investment represents only 20 percent of the total expenditure. The true cost of IT can accurately be estimated by multiplying the apparent cost by five.

DIRECT CAPITAL INVESTMENT

Direct capital investment costs are tracked by traditional accounting systems. Because the costs of facilities, equipment, direct investment, working capital, and the like appear on the balance sheet, they may be easier to find than some other costs, but allocating them accurately to specific processes can be difficult. It is essential, for instance, to distinguish between capital investment that is directly related to process activity and fixed enterprise costs. If a firm was to outsource, say, its tax compliance processes, some facility costs might be reduced, but others—such as the main computer center—would probably stay at the same level. The best way to estimate the direct capital investment attributable to a process is to work backwards and to ask what reduction in capital investment would result from abandoning or outsourcing the process.

INDIRECT CAPITAL INVESTMENT

Empty offices owned by a company consume capital. When a firm downsizes, or when it outsources or streamlines a process in a way that leads to layoffs, the cost of maintaining unused space should be attributed to the process and should figure in the cost-benefit analysis. In practice, the connection between processes and such indirect capital costs tends to get blurred or erased.

PROCESS VALUE MINUS TRUE CAPITAL COST EQUALS TRUE VALUE

My emphasis on the importance of developing reasonably accurate estimates of the capital tied up in major processes is grounded in the concept of EVA, which measures a firm's long-term prosperity. It is neither a process's soft benefits nor simply the earnings or apparent profits these benefits generate that classify the process as an asset or a liability. These factors do not indicate whether it contributes to or threatens the success of a firm. To repeat, a process can be considered an asset *only* if it increases a firm's value by generating a positive cash flow after the cost of the capital has been deducted. A negative cash flow makes a process a liability, regardless of the benefits it seems to provide.

KINDS OF ASSET PROCESSES

The cash-flow approach to determining whether processes are assets or liabilities needs a little qualification. Three kinds of processes should be considered assets, even though only one of them *directly* generates economic value.

1. **VALUE-GENERATING PROCESSES.** These are the processes that clearly provide something of value to customers or that generate value for the firm itself by reducing costs and improving margins. Marketing, manufacturing, and pricing are examples of value-generating processes. If you answer yes to the question "Does this process directly contribute to our after-tax cash flow after the cost of the capital tied up in it is subtracted?" then the process is a value-generating asset.

2. **OPTION-ENABLING PROCESSES.** These give a firm an advantage in dealing with uncertainty and change. Although they may not be directly value-generating, they put the firm in a position to exploit new value-generating opportunities. They enhance corporate flexibility, speed up response and learning, sharpen focus, and encourage shared commitment. Research and design, education, team-building, and planning are examples of option-enabling processes. For instance, Shell's development of scenario-planning processes is widely seen as an important source of the firm's ability to respond quickly and effectively to political, social, and economic change. If you answer yes to the question "Does this process help make sure we keep ahead?" then the process is an option-enabling asset.

3. **VALUE-PRESERVING PROCESSES.** Neglecting these processes reduces the company's ability to compete and to continue to generate economic value. Such processes may not create economic value directly, but not having them would result in value loss. Many advertising and customer support processes fall into this category. Over time, some value-generating processes become value-preserving ones. For instance, automated teller machines generated value when only a few banks had them and they provided a competitive advantage. Now that they are universal, they are required to preserve value. If you answer yes to the question "Is this process intrinsic, not peripheral, to supporting our value-generating processes?" then the process is a value-preserving asset. In many cases, improving these processes will result in more value being generated by the processes they support.

EVA, NOT PROFITS

Reviewing salience in the previous chapter, I said that investors' valuations are the ones that count most. It is virtually impossible to overestimate the importance of the investor's view of company value. According to Alfred Rappaport, "Those who criticize the goal of value maximization are forgetting that stockholders are not merely the beneficiaries of the corporation's financial success, but also the referees who determine management's financial power. Any management—no matter how powerful and independent—that flouts the financial objective of maximizing shareholder value does so at its own peril."[4] Whether or not they are aware of a process's details, investors judge its effects by the company's performance—its ability to create rather than consume wealth. EVA is based on this concept of shareholder value as the real measure of a company's worth and its processes.

Peter Drucker neatly articulates the connections among capital, profits, EVA, and shareholder value:

EVA is based on something we have known for a long time: what we generally call profits, the money left to service equity, is usually not profit at all. Until a business returns a profit that is greater than its cost of capital, it operates at a loss. Never mind that it pays taxes as if it had a genuine profit. The enterprise still returns less to the economy than it devours in resources. It does not cover its full cost unless the reported profit exceeds the cost of capital. Until then, it does not create wealth; it destroys it. By that measurement, incidentally, few U.S. businesses have been profitable since World War II.[5]

This description suggests that firms can report profits and pay taxes on those profits while the real value of the company is decreasing. If we assume that profits equal wealth, this will seem paradoxical. The paradox disappears, however, as soon as we understand that profits do not represent real value if the cost of generating them is too high. Some examples drawn from Bennett Stewart's *The Quest for Value* illustrate the point.[6]

In 1992, Spiegel, the catalog retailer, reported an operating profit of $188 million. After paying $69 million in taxes, the firm had a net profit of $119 million, a respectable 7.5 percent return on assets. But the total capital Spiegel used to generate this return was $1.6 billion. Its weighted average cost of capital—a combination of interest rates for debt and the cost of equity—was 11.1 percent in 1992, or $178 million. The firm was profitable but suffered a net value loss of $59 million.

IBM's performance in 1988 tells a similar story. The firm's return on assets was around 10 percent, but its weighted average cost of capital was close to 13 percent. IBM's value loss was $1.7 billion that year. Investors were not blind to the problem. They valued the company at $80 billion, although this represents a market value-added (MVA) of $20 billion over IBM's capital base of $60 billion—a $26 billion drop in MVA from the 1983 figure. By 1993, MVA had plunged $75 billion from its earlier high. By contrast, Wal-Mart, which had essentially the same cost of capital as IBM, generated a 25 percent return on that capital in 1988. Its MVA on a capital base of $5 billion was $20 billion—a $9 billion increase since 1983.

Fundamental to EVA is the idea that cash is the only real basis of value. Free cash flow is the operating profit minus the cost of all the capital used to generate it. One of the corollaries of this cash-value theory is that a firm's value and the valuation of its stock can actually increase when reported profits are reduced. How is this possible? Let's start with an example from personal rather than corporate finances.

Say that we buy an item costing $10,000. We have to pay $10,000 for it whether we can deduct it from our taxes or not, but our after-tax cash flow—the real measure of our added wealth—looks very different at the end of the year in the two cases. Being able to deduct the $10,000 reduces gross adjusted income, the individual equivalent of a corporation's before-tax profits, and increases after-tax cash flow, the free cash flow that is real money in the sense that you have it available to spend or save as you wish. Assuming for the sake of convenience a 30 percent marginal tax rate and an adjusted gross income of $40,000, here is the difference between not deducting and deducting that $10,000 purchase:

	No deduction	Deduction
Adjusted gross income	$40,000	$40,000
Deductions	0	$10,000
Pretax earnings	$40,000	$30,000
Tax	$12,000	$9,000
After-tax "profit"	$28,000	$21,000
Cash in hand (gross – tax – the $10,000 purchase)	$18,000	$21,000

Without the deduction, earnings on paper are more than 30 percent higher, but real added wealth is 14 percent less. Although this example is simple, it illustrates a valid truth: that lower reported profits can increase value.

The same phenomenon has been observed when companies changed their inventory accounting method from "first in first out" (FIFO) to "last in first out" (LIFO). FIFO assumes that the item the firm has just sold is the oldest in its inventory and therefore usually the cheapest. LIFO assumes that the item is the most recent—typically the most expensive. The shift from FIFO to LIFO has no impact on what the firm paid for its inventory. If it paid $800 for an item in 1994 and $1,200 for the same item in 1995, it spent $2,000 on the two items, regardless of which it expenses first when it makes a sale. But expensing the $1,200 item first decreases the margin between cost and selling price and reduces reported profits. As in the preceding personal finances example, this reduces the company's tax liability and increases its cash flow and hence its shareholder value. As Figure 4-2 shows, firms that switched to LIFO did increase their market value, whereas firms that increased profits by switching to FIFO lost value.

The market reacted similarly to R.J. Reynolds when the tobacco firm's managers went on an earnings binge in the late 1980s. RJR offered distributors incentives to stock up on cigarette inventory near the end of 1988, boosting reported sales and profits. When RJR was preparing to introduce its semiannual price increase in 1989, in its stock were more than 18 billion cigarettes that had been sold to distributors at a lower price and on which the company had already paid excise tax. And when you add the fact that cigarettes become stale after a time, the ineffectiveness of RJR's earnings strategy is beyond dispute. The company soon paid the price: shipments dropped 29 percent in the third quarter, compared with the previous year, and 19 percent in the fourth quarter. RJR's stock, however, went up when these results became known. The company stopped the discounting policy and stopped trying to buy profits today at tomorrow's expense. Investors saw the company as thus taking actions to restore real economic value rather than to generate paper profits that actually increased its liabilities.[7]

THE COST OF CAPITAL

As the Spiegel example shows, EVA is based on the carrying cost of capital, some of which derives from the interest paid on corporate debt. The cost of equity capital is the investors' opportunity cost—the share price they are willing to pay to benefit from the firm's present and future value. Despite the common criticism that Wall Street puts too much emphasis on short-term gains, there is persuasive evidence that most investors look for lasting value, not just earnings. With the obvious exception of speculators, investors

FIGURE 4-2

LOWER REPORTED PROFITS INCREASE MARKET VALUE

Cumulative returns vs. market

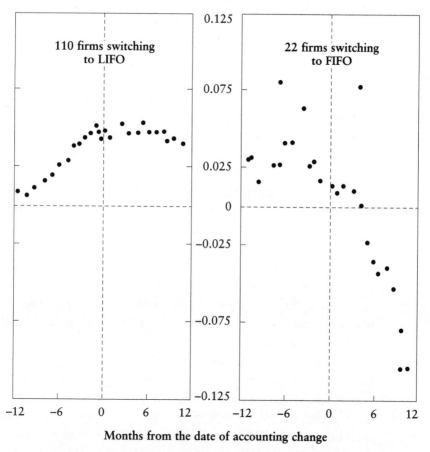

Months from the date of accounting change

SOURCE: S. Sunder, "The Relationship Between Accounting Changes and Stock Prices: Problems of Measurement and Some Empirical Evidence," *Empirical Research in Accounting: Selected Studies* (1973): 18.

hold stock as long as they believe the value of a company meets or exceeds the value of their investment.

The cost of borrowed capital is easy to understand: it equals the cost of servicing the debt incurred. The impact of the interest rate paid on real value as opposed to profit can be shown in another modest example. Say a friend invested $25,000 in short-term securities and has earned a 10 percent return at a time when you were getting 3 percent on the $25,000 you invested in certificates of deposit. You would probably be impressed, but your admiration would fade if you discovered that your friend had borrowed the $25,000 on credit cards at an 18 percent annual interest rate. From an EVA perspective, the after-tax result of the investment would be $1,750 (assuming a 30 percent tax rate), minus the after-tax interest on the credit card loan of $3,150. The $2,500 return on investment is real but meaningless. The EVA is a negative $1,400 because the cost of capital is higher than the value it generated. Your friend's wealth is decreased because the cost of the capital he invested was higher than the profit that capital generated. (If your friend had financed the deal by investing his $25,000 bonus check instead of paying off his credit card balance, the cost of capital would have been the same. His "opportunity cost" would have been the credit card interest rate he could have saved.)

The cost of a firm's equity capital is the minimum rate of return that investors expect from the company—a figure implicit in its current stock price. Because investors always have the option of putting their money elsewhere, that figure represents the true cost of equity capital—the value the firm must create to meet investors' expectations. Earnings per share are part of this value, but so are product introductions, joint ventures, announcements about research and development, and other factors that investors use to judge a company's present and future value. The cost of equity capital is higher than the cost of borrowed capital because the return on borrowed capital is generally guaranteed. Junk bonds issued by companies with weak balance sheets offer investors the potential of high return in exchange for high risk. This connection between risk and promised return underlies the rule of thumb for determining the cost of capital that I described earlier. For an investor, equity is inherently riskier than secured loans, so the cost of capital is higher.

That earnings are only one of the factors that determine value is demonstrated in the example of McCaw, the cellular telecommunications firm that AT&T acquired in 1993 for close to $13 billion. McCaw spent its capital building a presence across the country by purchasing licenses to operate cellular telephone services in major metropolitan areas. The going price for these licenses was well below what they would be worth when and if the cellular phone market took off. Although the company had never made a profit, McCaw shareholders and AT&T considered the potential value of these licenses worth more than current earnings. In fact, as Figure 4-3 indicates, there is no correlation between market value and reported earnings, but there is a strong connection between market value and EVA. In late 1993, the chairman of AT&T said, "We calculated our EVA back to 1984 and found an almost perfect correlation with stock price."[8]

EVA AND PROCESS INVESTMENT

It should be evident by now that Peter Drucker's definition of EVA for a business applies to the processes in that business: until a process returns a profit that is greater than its cost of capital, it is a liability. Proposals for process changes—whether called reengineering, total quality management, process redesign, "rightsizing," or simply "change"—must be based on the economics of capital. Too many process movement advocates talk as if capital were free. In the real world, though, capital is scarce and expensive and must be divided among many conflicting and even competing business needs and opportunities. The only justification for diverting capital from, say, advertising, plant expansion, or acquisitions to business process investments is that doing so makes better use of that capital—that is, it generates more EVA.

The benefits created by reengineering and other process improvements may in fact add economic value, but managers and process consultants need to focus on creating value—the real goal of process investment—and not make the mistake of thinking that process benefits are the goal. Business process reengineering is prone to that error, as was its direct forerunner, IT-for-competitive-advantage. Both IT and process gurus have mistaken means for ends and have simply assumed that process improvements automatically resulted in added value. By and large, they have been blind to the economic realities of process investment.[9] They have

FIGURE 4-3

THERE IS ZERO CORRELATION BETWEEN ACCOUNTING PROFITS AND SHARE PRICE

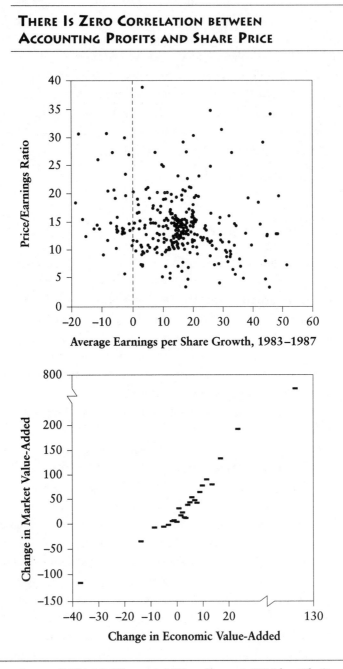

SOURCE: Exhibit 5.8: "Changes in MVA vs. Changes in EVA" from *The Quest for Value* by G. Bennett Stewart. Copyright © by Ballinger Publishing Company. Reprinted by permission of HarperCollins Publishers, Inc.

not paid adequate attention to the true cost of processes or process reform and have generally defined *benefits* in terms of improvements in processes, not value added to the firm. In the mid-1980s, when the competitive advantage supposedly offered by IT was a hot topic, it was argued that IT investment would lead to business success through such technology payoffs as "better" planning and "improved" customer service. Too often, however, the actual results were huge IT investments that produced no discernible economic payoff and extravagant praise of firms whose innovative use of IT was supposed to have given them a striking competitive advantage but did not.

These experts—myself among them—pointed to American Hospital Supply, Citibank, Merrill Lynch & Co., and American Airlines as examples of firms that would reap the benefits of the new technologies. We largely ignored Wal-Mart, although in retrospect it stands out for its use of IT to transform its distribution system. Wal-Mart is not mentioned in *20/20 Vision, Competing Against Time,* or my own *Competing in Time: Using Telecommunications for Competitive Advantage.*[10] Most of the success stories we told instead have not fared nearly as well in the marketplace.

How could so many of us whose job it is to alert managers to what is happening in business and technology have overestimated IT's impact on some firms and overlooked its importance to others, missing the Wal-Mart phenomenon entirely through most of the 1980s? The main reason is that we concentrated on the means— information technology—and believed that the ends would take care of themselves. The IT movement assumed, incorrectly, that technological improvements would pay off. It completely ignored the economics of capital.

In *The Quest for Value,* Stewart says, "Kick the earnings habit. Join the cash flow generation."[11] Process investment says, "Kick the benefits habit." *Benefits* is a managerial concept; *value* is an economic concept. A writer may call a firm an exemplar of "excellence," laud its use of IT for "competitive advantage," or describe the benefits of its reengineering projects, but none of this answers two key investor questions: Does all this excellence actually increase the value of the firm? What operational indicators would demonstrate the existence of added value to outside observers?

Only appropriate answers to these questions will lead investors to bid up the firm's market value.

In other words, business process reform and investment genuinely benefits a company only when it increases EVA. Process changes can add economic value in three basic ways:

- They reduce the capital that the process ties up by eliminating it, outsourcing it, or streamlining it.
- They get more value from an existing process by making investments that improve service, quality, and coordination or turn the process into a value-generating product or franchise.
- They invest new capital to generate new value by reengineering the entire process base, combining separate processes, or creating new processes.

WHEN BENEFITS DO MEAN VALUE

Although there is no simple answer to the question of how to determine when the benefits of process improvement really create value, here are a few guidelines for assessing the most common of these benefits.

- **REDUCED TIME.** The value of reducing time and steps should be apparent in such metrics as revenues and profit per employee, one of the most reliable measures of productivity. MCI, which has made speed a competitive priority, generates $355,000 in sales and nearly $19,000 in profit per employee, compared with Bellsouth Corp.'s respective figures of $165,000 and $11,000.
- **QUALITY.** Short-term value metrics include reductions in warranty costs, reworking costs, and waste. Long-term metrics are harder to define but include market share and published evaluations by organizations that rate quality, such as *Consumer Reports* and J. D. Powers.
- **DOWNSIZING.** The main metrics here are employee-based measures of productivity: revenues and profit per employee. Unless these increase, there is no economic justification for downsizing. Even when they do improve, the economic costs

of severance, retraining, and reorganization must be included in the EVA analysis. Human costs are more complex. Few metrics exist to quantify the economic effects of reduced morale, management credibility, and trust.

- **CUSTOMER SERVICE.** Customer retention rates are the main value metric.

- **REDUCED INVENTORIES AND BACKLOGS.** The economic value of benefits created by process change is relatively easy to measure in terms of unit cost, turnover per day (or per square foot or per store), and the like.

EVA IN ACTION

In a September 1993 article on EVA, *Fortune* concluded that "managers who run their businesses according to the precepts of EVA have hugely increased the value of their companies."[12] Firms that have used EVA to guide their business process decisions have had some notable successes.

CSX adopted EVA as its guide for making major business process changes in 1988. The railroad firm has a lot of capital tied up in its operations, primarily the massive costs of locomotive equipment. By using EVA to understand the economics of its processes, it increased freight volume by 25 percent while reducing the number of containers and trailers it used by more than 20 percent. It saved $70 million in capital by cutting its locomotive fleet from 150 to 100. It did this by intentionally *reducing* the efficiency of its train operation processes. This "improvement" seems directly contrary to the process movement emphasis on increased efficiency and the almost universal belief that speed is a competitive advantage. But CSX saw that when its trains traveled at 28 miles an hour, they arrived at their destinations around midnight and were not unloaded until morning. When their speed was cut to 25 miles an hour, fuel consumption was cut by 25 percent and the number of trains needed was reduced from four to three. They arrived later but were unloaded at the same time. Similar attention to the scheduling of containers and trailers, a priority process for CSX, cut the number needed from 18,000 to 14,000, again reducing CSX's cost of capital. As *Fortune* noted, "They used to sit in terminals for two weeks between runs, but once CSX started seeing them as idle capital, they figured out ways to return them to the rails in five days. This is hardly rocket science. But before EVA, no one had had enough incentive to do so."[13] When CSX first adopted EVA, its stock price was $30 per share. Six years later it was more than $90 per share. As CSX's chief executive officer explained it, "How we use capital determines market value."[14] More precisely, how they use capital determines EVA, which determines market value.

EVA analysis convinced equipment manufacturer Briggs and Stratton to outsource many of its manufacturing processes because they did earn back the cost of capital invested in them. The firm's 1990 return on capital was less than 8 percent, and its cost of capital was 12 percent. By 1993, its outsourcing strategy had helped to increase the rate of return to more than 12 percent, and the company's stock rose from $20 per share in 1990 to around $50 per share in early 1994.

Coca-Cola Co.'s return on assets in the mid-1980s was one-half of its 16 percent cost of capital. Adopting EVA led directly to the abandonment of many capital projects and operations. The firm's chief executive officer succinctly described the firm's EVA approach: "We raise capital to make concentrate, and sell it at an operating profit. Shareholders pocket the difference."[15] Coca-Cola's 1995 per-employee sales were $483,000, and its per-employee profits were $76,000 (compared with an industry median of $215,000 and $14,000, respectively). Its stock price moved from less than $5 per share in the 1980s to just under $60 per share in 1995.

Using EVA, these companies discovered which of their major processes were economic liabilities and could be abandoned or outsourced. They determined which processes could generate additional value when the amount of capital tied up in them was reduced and which were assets that deserved more capital investment. They based their decisions on the real costs and real economic value of their processes and were therefore successful at a time when many other firms got no real benefit from the process reforms that were supposed to give them a competitive advantage.

Next Steps

Now that we have looked at the main issues involved in determining process salience and worth, it should be practical for managers to develop a process portfolio for their firms, eliminating the many value-neutral processes that fill the process swamp and positioning the remaining key processes on the salience/worth matrix. Managers especially need to strive for a clear sense of which are the company's identity and priority processes and whether these are assets or liabilities. My discussion of EVA has, I hope, amply demonstrated the importance of basing process investment (and divestment) decisions on their potential for adding economic value.

Having completed these essential steps, I now move on to the specific actions appropriate to different processes in different circumstances. These actions, all of which aim to increase the EVA of business processes, are the value builders I described briefly in Chapter 1 and will consider in detail in the following chapters.

CHAPTER 5

PROCESS VALUE BUILDERS

ABANDON OR ADJUST

ONCE A FIRM'S MANAGERS KNOW WHICH OF ITS BUSINESS processes tie up sufficient capital to make them part of its process portfolio and worthy of further attention, they can begin to determine which process value builders should be applied to them. I discuss the process value builder options roughly in order of risk and complexity, beginning with what are typically the most conservative, low-risk actions and proceeding to the most radical and far-reaching kinds of change.

This order can be reversed. The "right" procedure is largely a question of corporate philosophy and culture. Reengineering typically takes a radical approach, whereas total quality management aims to arrive at major improvement through sustained incremental change. Whether a firm is thinking incrementally or radically, however, the sensible starting point is to ask if a particular process should be carried out at all. Abandoning a process is far cheaper than redesigning or reengineering it.

ABANDON: IF A JOB'S NOT WORTH DOING, DON'T DO IT

Because they serve no purpose and provide no value, folklore processes should of course automatically be abandoned. The creation of reports that no one uses, the cumbersome procedures that persist long after the conditions that justified them change, and all the processes carried out solely because "we've always done this" should simply be stopped. They drain value and may distract the organization from genuinely important concerns.

After folklore processes, the most likely candidates for abandonment are inessential background liabilities. Years ago, a giant European petrochemical firm abandoned travel-expense account reporting, a background liability process that consumed the time of the traveler and added to the costs incurred by the travel department and the company's accountants and auditors. Instead, along with their plane tickets, business travelers were given a cash per diem in the currency of the country they were visiting. The firm arranged for company limousines to take them to and from airports to resolve the problem of the cost differentials in different locations. If travelers did not spend all the cash, the surplus was theirs to keep, as was the responsibility of reporting additional taxable income. If they ran short, they were likely to make up the difference on another trip.

Processes that consume capital in the form of facilities, staff, and information technology (which, remember, can require capital investment equal to five times its direct cost) and generate little value can be abandoned, provided that doing so does not generate extra costs for the firm or create unacceptable risks. One casualty and property insurance company decided in 1992 that applying its full claims adjustment process to small claims was largely a liability: the cost of handling the claims was higher than the amount of the claims. The full process, which involved a complex set of steps to build a case file, created delays for the customer as well as expense for the company; this was a priority process for handling major claims because the firm's profitability depends largely on its loss ratios—the percentage of premiums it pays back in claims. In the case of small claims, however, the company reasoned that abandoning the adjustment process would reduce expenses without having much effect on the loss ratio. Instead of going through the whole complex process, experienced adjusters could scan the small-claims documents to weed out fraudulent or dubious claims and authorize immediate payment of those that looked legitimate.

The company needed to make sure, though, that abandoning the process did not encourage fraud or reduce adjusters' vigilance. It knew it would have to monitor the volume of claims and possible changes in loss ratios to make sure that discontinuing a liability process did not lead to a greater liability. Financial control officers worried about a drift from uncontrolled very small claims to uncontrolled small ones to uncontrolled substantial claims. The firm resolved the risk implicit in the change by looking at it in terms of EVA. It calculated (1) the reduction in capital costs resulting from not applying the full adjustment process to small claims, (2) the extra capital cost incurred by faster payment of claims, and (3) the additional business created through rapid settlement. It estimated that its enhanced reputation for service would lead to a 2 percent increase in new policy sales and a 3 percent gain in renewals. The results of the calculations led senior management to conclude that the benefits of abandoning the process more than offset the potential risks.

Abandoning a process generates EVA by virtue of the fact that most or all of the capital tied up in it is eliminated. This can also create new economic value when it improves the customer's perception of the firm's quality or service, as in the case of the insurance company. Reducing the number of processes that managers have to coordinate can simultaneously save money and make the firm more effective. A major consequence of today's global economy, variety of customer demands, and continuing waves of changes is organizational complexity. Complexity is not the same as size, although the two are related. Large firms especially have responded to growing environmental complexity by increasing their own organizational complexity. Now, in Rosabeth Moss Kanter's phrase, these elephants must learn to dance. Giant firms must become more flexible and swift, reducing bureaucracy and its associated costs. One way to do this is to abandon processes that do not justify the corporate attention and capital invested in them, thereby replacing complexity with simplicity.

Many firms will have at least some background processes that can be eliminated. Because of legal requirements, mandated processes cannot be abandoned. Identity processes and the priority processes that support them should almost never be abandoned (except as a crisis survival move): they are more likely to be candidates for improvement. Occasionally, though, an identity liability and the priority processes that exist because of it can be profitably done away with. My own experience in managing my small consulting and research firm provides an example.

The firm's activities included publishing books through its own press. The books were well-researched, innovative, and well-received by the academic community. The direct costs of publishing were relatively low, with a break-even point on sales of only a few thousand copies. Book publishing looked like an identity asset in the sense that it made a positive contribution to the firm's reputation. From an EVA point of view, however, it was a significant liability. Research required years of effort and incurred costs far greater than those of direct publishing. Writing took up a significant fraction of the author's time, and editing absorbed even more of the staff's time. Order processing, distribution, and inventory management added to the burden. The publishing process was skilfully executed, but a liability process is not necessarily one that is carried out incompetently. It may just be the wrong process for a particular organization or business environment. Because the publishing activities worked well, I was oblivious to their real cost for some time. Had they been badly handled, I would have realized sooner just how much of an economic drain they were. Viewed in terms of direct costs, the publishing endeavor broke even and enhanced the organization's image. Viewed in terms of capital investment, it drained value.

Closing down the operation restored value. It did affect the company's identity, making it less of an academic enterprise and more of a consulting firm. If this change had led to a decline in consulting contracts, then publishing would have proved to be an essential identity process. As a generator of consulting revenue as well as publishing revenue, it would have been an asset, not a liability. As it happened, the shift in identity did not affect the firm's reputation, so the decision to abandon publishing was the right one.

OUTSOURCE: ONE FIRM'S BACKGROUND LIABILITY IS ANOTHER'S IDENTITY ASSET

Most companies evaluate outsourcing mainly in terms of systems and facilities, relative costs, and whether the functions being considered for outsourcing are strategic to the firm. There is, for instance, extensive literature on the reasons for and against outsourcing information services groups and data centers. I suggest looking at outsourcing in terms of processes rather than facilities or groups, and considering it as a form of business process investment, with an obvious focus on reducing economic liabilities.

Outsource background and mandated processes to firms *for whom they are identity assets.* The most likely candidates are processes that have well-defined boundaries and therefore require little active coordination from within. Naturally, there must also be proven providers available whose reputations rest on handling these processes well—that is, firms who have turned these processes into their products and identity assets. Such firms are increasing in number and generally specialize in narrowly focused processes that they seek to execute skillfully and cost-efficiently. Common examples are payroll, office cleaning and plant care, security, printing services, distribution, and telephone and mail-order fulfillment.

For the clothing and textile retailer Laura Ashley, distribution is a background process that was a distinct liability: only 65 percent of its shipments to stores arrived on time. An executive described the delivery system as "complex, costly, and inefficient." In 1992 the company outsourced its entire supply process, including warehousing and store delivery, to Business Logistics, a subsidiary of Federal Express. Efficient and reliable small-package delivery is among Federal Express's identity assets, and it turned these assets into a product by creating Business Logistics. What for Laura Ashley was a poorly executed and value-draining background process, unrelated to the identity processes of its fabric design, is the main focus and source of value for Business Logistics.

Although Laura Ashley seems to have resolved its faulty distribution, it faces other, more critical problems. At the time it signed a ten-year contract with Business Logistics, its design processes had lost touch with consumer tastes. Its margins were dropping and its losses increasing. It needed to change its mix of stores and locations. Outsourcing distribution will not in itself make the company successful, although it should help protect operating margins by reducing the cost of distribution as a percentage of sales—a figure investors track closely. The EVA of the company's outsourcing decisions should be substantial: up to a 20 percent reduction in warehouse inventory, a direct and visible capital cost; a reduction of 10 to 12 percent in distribution costs; and capital savings of $5 million that the firm would otherwise have spent to upgrade its software systems for inventory-distribution processes.

British Petroleum has aggressively outsourced background processes. In the late 1980s, it went through a major management and organizational shakeout that included the forced resignation of the company's chairman. The new leadership took a hard look at the firm and saw an organization that was too complex and diffuse. British Petroleum's identity asset processes had historically been in the area of exploration. Why, then, management asked, was its exploration unit spending such a large proportion of its resources on running large computer data centers? The decision was made to outsource the data services that the unit had been handling. As one executive said, "We're in the business of finding oil. There are plenty of people who are in the business of computing. Let them compute for us."[1] British Petroleum chose to outsource these computer services to capitalize on vendor expertise more than to save money.

Outsourcing computer data services has become common. British Petroleum's decision to outsource all of its management accounting and tax-compliance processes is more unusual. The company reasoned that these processes would generate little value even if carried out as efficiently as possible. Value can come from the firm's *use* of information supplied by management accounting processes. The firm chose to retain planning, decision-making, and performance monitoring as priority processes but to farm out the underlying background processes to a top public accounting firm for whom those processes are identity assets. British Petroleum chose Arthur Andersen as its supplier of accounting and tax-compliance services, again basing its choice on expertise rather than cost.

Companies have been implicitly applying the principle of outsourcing background liability processes for years. For example, many companies have their catering done by outside firms for whom that service is an identity asset. They use recruiting firms for hiring, especially for the priority process of acquiring senior executives. An outside recruiting firm can generate more EVA for the company than would result from handling the process in house. The EVA may come from the savings that result from not maintaining capital-consuming staff and facilities, or it may derive from the better results that a first-rate executive search firm is likely to produce. Although outsourcing is a value builder usually applied to background and mandated processes, in some circumstances even a priority process may be profitably outsourced. The deciding factor is always how best to generate value.

Freeze the Process or System and Fix the Front End

Front-ending leaves the core of a complex process alone and finds ways to moderate its flaws and limitations by changing the parts that are closest to the customer or to the employees who interact with it. The strategy is mainly applicable to processes that depend on complex mainframe computer systems. Rebuilding these legacy systems from the ground up is often not practical. Use front-ending to reduce the costs and stresses of reengineering when the process relies heavily on old and inefficient computer systems.

The word *legacy* suggests the analogy of a wealthy aunt's leaving you a palace on a picturesque hillside in Italy, but, to the contrary, these massive old computer software complexes are ancestral curses: they are more like a vengeful uncle's burdening you unto the tenth generation with a palace sinking into the canals of Venice and becoming a tremendous tax liability. The effort to reengineer the processes these systems serve—or, rather, impede—is blocked by legacy systems. Rebuilding them is sometimes impossible: most are undocumented and were not systematically designed in the first place. Developing entirely new software and moving old records into a new system can costs millions or even billions of dollars. Even if that amount of money could be invested, the time required to create a new system would be prohibitive: business cannot be put on hold while years are spent developing new software. Reengineering legacy systems from scratch is a bit like deciding to reengineer the JFK International Airport by blowing it up. It may be a tempting idea, but it is not a practical one.

Legacy/curse systems will be with many companies for the rest of this century and beyond. Front-ending is the most practical way to make process improvements that these systems would otherwise prevent. Front-ending leaves legacy systems in place and uses telecommunications and computing capabilities to convert mainframe data into messages that workstations can handle.[2] System users, whether customers or staff, are shielded from the mainframe's complexity and rigidity by workstation software that is friendlier and more flexible. The process is in fact improved, although the same old machinery is chugging along behind the scenes. Furthermore, all new development for a front-ended system is done on workstations and intermediate machines: the role of the mainframe is gradually reduced, and the legacy system eventually fades away.

Making complex systems appear simple is a complex task, however. Think of the apparent simplicity of the front end of the public utility that provides electricity. The two- or three-pin interface that allows a user to plug in and dry his or her hair hides an extraordinarily complex infrastructure that has evolved over a century and requires billions of dollars for maintenance, enhancement, and operation. Companies are finding that front-ending information systems may look simple but often proves to be the corporate equivalent of the Tennessee Valley Authority electrification project of the 1930s. It requires superb technical and organizational skills.

Bell Atlantic, one of the most aggressive of the traditionally conservative Bell operating companies, provides an example of front-ending. Its customer-service and provisioning processes depend on software systems that are, in some cases, more than a quarter of a century old. These systems significantly limit the quality of service, but to start anew and do things right would cost perhaps $20 billion. Bell Atlantic's solution is to use workstations at the front end of the process, adding the needed functionality and flexibility here while the old systems continue to work in the background. It has budgeted $2.1 billion to make these improvements. Although this is a considerable sum, the company really has no other choice: the processes must be improved, and starting with a clean slate is out of the question. Front-ending gives Bell Atlantic an opportunity to redesign its central customer-service processes in some innovative ways. It will be able, for instance, to install workstations in public locations such as supermarkets, where a customer can talk with a service representative who will see to it that the service to which the customer has just subscribed—call forwarding or emergency dialing, for example—will be activated by the time he or she gets home.

Opportunities for front-ending may seem more limited than for other kinds of process improvement, but there are in fact many complex, work-flow–based processes that depend on and are often crippled by huge, antiquated systems. With the cost-effectiveness of computer hardware improving by about 40 percent per year, companies can afford to throw desktop computing power at the problems inherent in these processes. So front-ending can be an important process investment strategy for most large firms.

SELF-SOURCE: DO IT YOURSELF

A bank's ATMs provide a convenient service for customers, giving them access to their accounts at any time and at many locations. It also turns them (that is, us) into data-entry clerks for the bank. We key in information about our deposits and withdrawals and save the bank about 35 percent of what these transactions would cost if handled by a teller. Both the customer and the bank are happy. Get people out of the loop if the change increases customer convenience and reduces company cost.

Not all self-sourcing involves computers. Self-service gas stations, restaurant salad bars, and orchards where customers pick their own apples are examples of self-sourcing practices that do not depend on technology. Many self-sourcing opportunities, however—from ATMs to automated help desk inquiries to tax-form filing via touch-tone telephone—are made possible by computers and computer networks. Arno Penzias, the Nobel laureate, has explained the impact this technology can have on background processes, turning liabilities into assets and sometimes elevating them from background to priority or identity.[3] What I call the Penzias axiom states that any person or procedure that comes between a customer and a computer that can fully meet the customer's needs will, over time, be removed from the process. He points out that, before ATMs, bank tellers took customers' checks or deposit slips and entered the information into a computer via a teller workstation. Now the customer interacts directly with the computer. In the past, bank and securities firm customers who wanted to check their account balances used to contact a service agent who queried a computer system. Now customers use a phone (and sometimes a PC and a modem) to get the information directly from the same system in the form of synthesized voice output or as data displayed on their own monitors.

No figures are available on the overall savings firms derive from self-sourcing processes, but they are considerable. One bank calculated that it would have cost an extra $400 million per year if the transactions processed by ATMs in 1992 had been handled by tellers instead. Even the self-service salad bar reduces a restaurant's coordination and other process costs while giving the customer a lower price, more choice, and other benefits. The volume of work that can be successfully self-sourced to customers is sometimes immense. In the 1930s, analysts calculated that, given the growth rate in phone calls, by the 1960s every adult in the United States would have to be employed as an operator to connect all the parties who would be speaking to each other. That did not happen, of course. The technology of direct dialing allowed phone company customers to make those connections themselves.

Although electronic technology is not always involved in self-sourcing, computer workstations, portable computers with telecommunications capabilities, and touch-tone telephones have expanded firms' self-sourcing options. The recent explosive growth of the Internet is opening up new opportunities. The single most important feature of the Internet is not the World Wide Web, Gopher, Usenet, or FTP, but TCP/IP, the networking protocol that allows any computer of any type anywhere in the world to connect to any other computer. That universal connectivity means that a firm's transaction processing systems can talk to any customer's PC without either company or customer having to invest in telecommunications links or costly specialized software. All that is needed is a connection to the Internet by modem or other standard means.

Federal Express, so often a leader in exploiting technology for better service, is using the Internet to self-source package tracking. Package tracking has been one of its main competitive weapons for years, a way for the firm to differentiate itself from the U.S. Postal Service and UPS. Customers who phoned FedEx could find out exactly where their package was and when it would arrive at its destination. The company's first step in self-sourcing the process was to provide its biggest customers with workstations at no cost, shifting to those customers the work of weighing and labeling, informing FedEx when packages needed to be picked up, and tracking their delivery. Customers benefited from the convenience and immediate access to information that an in-house system offered. Because the process required use of Federal Express's own telecommunications network and was therefore quite expensive, it had to be limited to the highest-volume customers. The ubiquitous and much less expensive Internet has opened up the tracking service to all customers who have a PC and a modem. They gain, and so does Federal Express.

Often the "customer" who self-sources a process is an internal one—an employee who benefits from performing a function that had been provided by others in the company. For instance, it is more convenient, in most cases, to use a laptop to design your own presentation, write your own report, and send your own faxes than to have to go through the graphics department, the typing pool (an endangered group that once occupied whole floors of office buildings), or the cable department. At the same time, the reduced demand for such service departments cuts company costs.

Often it is both cheaper for the firm and more convenient for its sales representatives if those employees do not have an office. The firm saves on many background liability processes, including office cleaning, furniture purchasing, real estate management, security, and utility management. The sales reps can operate from their own homes or even their cars, using laptops or notebook computers, cellular phones, modems, and portable printers. The time they would have spent driving to the office to pick up messages and handle transactions can be used instead to visit customers. Self-sourcing and outsourcing can complement each other in such situations. Many companies now maintain satellite offices to which sales reps can come if they need to hold meetings or see customers in an office environment. Companies such as Headquarters specialize in running such offices for their corporate clients, providing secretarial, reception, and all of the other services associated with a business office. You can walk in, take a nameplate out of your briefcase, slide it into a slot on the door, and have your own office for a few hours.

Self-sourcing, with or without outsourcing, can improve productivity while dramatically reducing staffing needs. I myself cut the staff of my small research and consulting firm from fifty-five to five and increased both revenues and profits at the same time. The firm relied on two individuals to lead the projects, which involved substantial library research and the production of presentations and reports. The staff of fifty-five who supported this work included a receptionist, an accounting group, desktop publishing and editorial personnel, junior consultants, secretaries, research assistants, supervisors, and ancillary employees. A number of self-sourcing and outsourcing decisions made it possible to shrink the staff by more than 90 percent. Using on-line databases, senior staff could locate information directly, eliminating the need for research assistants. PC-based graphics and desktop publishing packages allowed us to generate our own presentations and reports. In fact, it was faster to design presentations this way than to lay out slides by hand, coordinate with the graphics group, correct their work, and so on. Outsourcing office functions to Headquarters and accounting and tax processes to firms that specialize in them resulted in a far more productive, efficient organization than the larger one had been. Although supported by a much smaller staff, I got much more work done, using technology-based self-sourcing and outsourcing to get the benefits of other companies' identity expertise. Very often, I pay far more in direct expenses for outside services than I paid to staff, but from an EVA perspective, this has added value to the firm because my own time is part of the real capital cost of operation.

At a time when most companies are aggressively trying to cut costs while improving productivity and service, leveraging the time and skills of key staff has become a priority for both the firm and staff members themselves. Juliet Shor's *Overworked Americans* demonstrates that on average we are working a thirteenth month a year compared with Americans in the 1950s: such are the results of the competitive pressures of the cruel economy.[4] Downsizing typically leads to increased workloads and reduced resources for those who keep their jobs. They must either work harder or more productively, or both. Self-sourcing can help them streamline their own work. Studies show that it is worth investing capital equal to 25 percent of a person's salary to gain him or her one extra hour of productive work a day.[5]

MODEST CHANGES, MAJOR BENEFITS

The value builders described in this chapter are process investment opportunities that generally do not involve rethinking the purpose, the nature, or, in some cases, the details of business processes. On one level, they add up to a kind of process housekeeping: tidying up processes without making major organizational changes or incurring significant risk. They are applicable most often to background processes. Abandoning, outsourcing, frontending, and self-sourcing are seldom appropriate strategies for improving priority processes and almost never can be employed with identity processes. (The example of my consulting firm abandoning the publishing process that was *part* of its identity is unusual.)

Nevertheless, these process adjustments can sometimes have important and highly visible effects. When Avis front-ended its rental car return processes, it raised the salience of a background process and generated benefits for itself and its customers. Previously, renters had to stand in line to pick up the piece of paper they needed for travel-expense reimbursement, or they dropped their rental agreements in a slot as they raced off to catch a plane. Now the company uses portable electronic devices to check in rental cars and print receipts on the spot while customers are taking their suitcases out of the trunk. For Avis, innovative front-ending turned a background liability into a priority asset.

CHAPTER 6

PROCESS VALUE BUILDERS

ENHANCE

Enhancing processes is an evolutionary strategy. The process value builders in this category generally require more lead time and capital investment than abandoning or adjusting processes, but they do not involve the kind of fundamental change that characterizes the value builders I discuss in Chapter 7. They also usually entail less risk than those more revolutionary strategies.

Although abandoning, outsourcing, and self-sourcing can often be accomplished without detailed knowledge of process steps, enhancement is built on an intimate knowledge of how specific processes work. Process enhancement makes use of techniques familiar from TQM and reengineering, both of which depend on thorough analyses of existing processes. Process enhancement differs from those movements in two ways, however. First, it can be applied to people-centered processes and not just the work flows on which reengineering in particular tends to concentrate. Second, like all process value builders, enhancements are evaluated in terms of EVA and not just the process improvements that may or may not create economic value.

STREAMLINE: REMOVE THE WASTE

Streamlining improves a process work flow by eliminating redundant tasks, material waste, lag time, unnecessary costs, and anything else that adds cost that does not contribute customer satisfaction. It is the typical approach of reengineering and TQM, and it can bring extensive improvements. Few organizations could not make improvements of 20 to 40 percent in at least one of their most costly and slow administrative processes. Streamlining to eliminate waste is at the core of Toyota's lean production, a process improvement that changed the basic principles of automobile manufacturing and was the foundation of TQM's success.

The processes best suited to streamlining mainly involve clear, linear sequences of activities with well-defined criteria for moving from one step to the next. Manufacturing, administrative, and production processes tend to be good candidates for streamlining. Design, research, and other processes that involve flexibility, judgment, and collaboration generally are not. The extensive literature on TQM describes many proven streamlining tools. They include statistical quality control, cause-and-effect diagrams, continuous incremental improvement (often referred to by the Japanese term *kaizen*), the Deming Wheel, and just-in-time inventory management. Total quality management has also engendered more specialized techniques such as the "Five Whys" of Toyota, the "House of Quality," concurrent engineering, the Taguchi loss function, and quality function deployment. (These terms are part of the essential vocabulary and discipline of TQM.)

Total quality management is well-grounded in theory and rigorously analytical, with a rich store of technique, insight, and experience. Because TQM offers the most effective streamlining tools, managers who choose streamlining as a process value builder will want to explore it in more detail than I can provide here. Its main principles offer valuable guidance for thinking about process enhancement:

- **EMBRACE THE LONG TERM.** Popular management books give a false idea of the time needed to transform companies through TQM. One of the least attractive and most damaging features of the reengineering movement is its contention that capable managers should try to transform their entire organizations immediately. The experience of TQM shows that streamlining basic manufacturing and service processes typically takes ten to fifteen years. There is no shortcut. If managers are not willing and able to make a sustained commitment of time, prestige, and effort, they should not embark on streamlining efforts. At a time when (in Carrie Fisher's phrase) the problem with instant gratification is that it is not fast enough, TQM requires more patience and perspective than many companies and managers can muster. It's better to outsource than to expect easy internal transformation.

- **GENUINELY EMPOWER WORKERS.** Whereas streamlining almost invariably displaces some workers, TQM teaches that managers must let go of the idea that they know best and instead harness the knowledge, initiative, and trust of the people who do the work. W. Edwards Deming, perhaps the single most influential figure in the TQM movement, believed that managers, not workers, were responsible for the erosion of U.S firms' competitiveness. He stressed the importance of teaching people how to work together and of building mutual trust. Empowering workers helps create the small changes that accumulate, over time, into major improvements.

- **REDUCE VARIABILITY.** This is the analytical and intellectual core of TQM, the principle behind many of its tools for gathering data, monitoring processes, and achieving quality goals.

- **MANAGE BY FACT.** Total quality management relies on observable fact, not opinion. Process performance is monitored and measured in precise, objective detail, with facts serving as the basis for problem identification and resolution.

- **REMOVE WASTE EVERYWHERE.** Total quality management is closely related to the just-in-time inventory management techniques that Toyota developed and used to reduce material, time, and labor waste.

- **GENERATE CONTINUOUS IMPROVEMENT.** A central tenet of TQM is that progress sustained over time adds up to dramatic improvement. The movement considers sustained incremental advances more practical than the great leap forward advocated by many reengineering proponents. Instead of aiming at, say, a 60 percent improvement in 2 years, TQM aims for a 10 percent annual improvement over the long term. Maintaining that rate would result in a 46 percent improvement at the end of the program's fifth year and a 236 percent improvement after 10 years.

THE ECONOMICS OF STREAMLINING

Streamlining a process, whether through TQM, reengineering, or some other process strategy, is likely to be costly. Management time, planning, staff training, displacement of workers, new incentives, and new systems require capital investment, as do the relatively long-term requirements for collecting process data, monitoring variations, and fine-tuning work flows that TQM involves. Because EVA is what matters, not process benefits per se, the cost of streamlining may outweigh the gains. A realistic determination of the capital tied up in this value builder and the potential economic gain it would produce may sometimes swing the investment strategy toward outsourcing or toward a decision to leave the process alone, despite its inefficiencies. It probably seems like heresy to tell a corporate community obsessed with time and time-based competition that a process may be good enough as is. Even in such industries as financial services, retailing, and manufacturing, where time often does mean EVA, streamlining may not generate enough value to make it the right process investment choice. The important issue is economics, not work flows. Think again of Mutual Benefit, which reduced the time it took to issue an insurance policy from three weeks to three hours but was taken over by regulators a few months after the publication of an article praising its process improvement. Investing in continuous improvement may make more sense for an identity or priority process than for a background one, unless streamlining raises the salience level of the background process. In Toyota's case, for example, streamlining manufacturing processes led to a level of quality and value that became part of Toyota's identity and therefore repaid the company's considerable investment of money and effort.

Obviously, it is unwise not to invest in a process that directly affects customer service. If however, it is a liability or does not build on what makes it a process asset, it is likely to be priority, not background, and to have a substantial effect on EVA. My heretical position here is analogous to the old maxim "If it ain't broke, don't fix it." If fixing it doesn't make a difference to EVA, invest the resources elsewhere.

HUB: BRING THE PROCESS TO ONE POINT

Hubbing brings work that had been spread across multiple departments and functions to one point. Hubbing is behind USAA's fabled superior service to its insurance clients, Dell Computer's customer service, Lands' End's retailing, and many other highly business-efficient and customer-satisfying processes. Hubbing is best suited to and can even transform decision-centered customer-service processes in which each unit traditionally handles only parts of the decision. Hubbing puts the whole decision in the hands of one employee. When a customer makes a purchase from Lands' End, one person takes the order, checks to see if the goods are in stock, passes the order on for fulfillment, and arranges payment. Similarly, any USAA customer-service representative can answer questions, add new policies or update existing ones, approve car loans, and provide other services. What had once been complex, multistage tasks are handled quickly and conveniently. USAA's hubbing turned administrative processes that are still background in most firms into priority and perhaps identity assets that customers see as unique in the industry. Both the firm and its customers benefit. In addition to enhancing its reputation, USAA realizes various kinds of savings. For instance, the company no longer sends customers printed copies of certain policies. Printing them would be a complex background liability process because of the length and detail of the documents and all the state-specific items that are required. Thanks to hubbing, customers don't demand printed policies. It is quicker and easier for them to phone the company to check on policy details than it would be to locate a printed policy and read it themselves.

Hubbing can dramatically expedite customer service. Merced County in California had a lengthy administrative process for new welfare applicants that involved separate applications at different state agency offices, fifteen or more forms to fill out, and interviews to schedule—all while the applicants were in critical situations. Once they had negotiated the complex process, they had to wait while their applications were checked against more than 2,500 state and federal government welfare rules, after which they would be asked to provide additional information in an interview. Typically, six weeks passed before the first payment was issued. After the process was transformed by hubbing, checks were usually issued in one day and never more than three days after the application was filed. The provider experienced a reduction in costs, and the customer saw an administrative nightmare turn into an efficient service.

Look at the customer's moment of value—the moment he or she wants a service—and work back from that point to develop a process that uniformly provides it. The moment of value for prospective house buyers occurs in the real estate office. They want to sign the offer on the spot but need to know if their mortgage will be approved. The moment of value typically passes without action. Instead, the buyers have to contact the bank during specific hours, fill out multiple copies of paper forms, and wait for the bank to coordinate a complex stream of procedures and come up with an answer. Citibank showed how to capture the moment of value through telephone access and customer-service workstations that turned mortgage approval into a fifteen-minute process. Unfortunately, the bank failed to build adequate risk management and quality control into its system. The software did not consistently filter out high-risk customers and properties and sometimes cut off solid prospects. Citibank's losses on the initiative were huge, but faulty execution does not negate the validity of its fresh thinking. I expect that another firm will replicate this service and make it work.

THE ROLE OF NETWORKED COMPUTERS

In many or most cases, reengineering cross-functional work flows to concentrate them at a single service point depends on computer networks and workstations to provide and process information. Historically, computers made elaborate work flows manageable and also created many of them. The U.S. federal tax system is an example of complexity that only computers can handle and that computers to some extent brought about. Networked desktop computers and workstations move in the opposite direction, encouraging simplicity. They replace the stream of documents that moved through departments and mail rooms and the small army of people needed to carry out multiple small process steps with on-line documentation instantly available to a single employee. They help provide services that, from the customer's point of view, are independent of time and location. Successfully hubbed customer service is like electricity—invisible to the customer, almost totally reliable, easy to access, and of general purpose. USAA's single 800 number, for example, handles all its customers' inquiries and requests.

Hubbing based on computer networking technology is responsible for a major shift in the organization of work and has demonstrated its worth as a provider of customer service at the moment of value. The extent to which companies can readily take advantage of hubbing depends on their information and transaction processing systems. Many existing IT systems are mutually incompatible. Unable to "talk" to each other, they cannot share information in the seamless way that makes hubbing work.[1] When hubbing is based on incompatible systems, the pieces of the process cannot be fully integrated. We can define the degree of integration in terms of reach and range. *Reach* refers to who can connect to a firm's service process and where that connection can be made. *Range* is a measure of how many kinds of information can be directly and automatically shared within the system. As Figure 6-1 makes clear, greater *reach* means easier access for the customer; greater *range* means complete service concentrated toward a single point and therefore greater efficiency. The two together make for convenient, fast, and responsive customer service.

FIGURE 6-1

THE BUSINESS DIMENSIONS OF THE IT PLATFORM

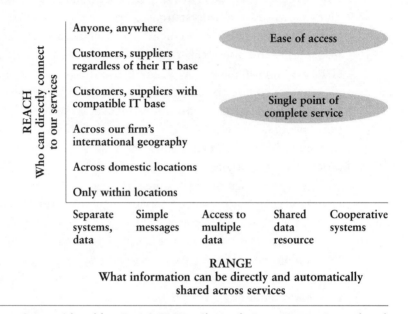

SOURCE: Adapted from Peter G. W. Keen, *Shaping the Future: Business Design through Information Technology* (Boston: Harvard Business School Press, 1991), 180.

Companies whose IT infrastructures lend themselves to hubbing stand out in their business environments. Like USAA, they have an opportunity to create value through process advantage. Firms hampered by IT incompatibilities will at some point have to make the tough decision to invest capital in hubbing to create—or eventually to preserve—value. The cost will be considerable in many cases. One major credit card company trying to hub processes for its five different card services expects to spend $55 million just for equipment and software. It will have to invest at least the same amount in managing the organizational changes and training needed to mesh culture and technology. Over five years, it will probably spend five times $55 million on operations, enhancements, and maintenance.

Hubbing and **EVA**

Hubbing is clearly a complex and long-term capital investment. As I made clear in the discussion of process worth and EVA, many of the capital costs may be hidden or ignored. Consider this example of hubbing in a managed health care firm. The initiative, which used image processing to reengineer a cumbersome paper-based insurance claims system, won an award from a leading IT publication in 1994. The reported benefits were impressive. A 30-day backlog was reduced so that claims were processed and paid in ten days, a little better than the industry average of 11.2. Staff was cut by 20 percent in the claims and customer-service departments. Errors in data entry shrank from 6 percent to 1.5 percent. The firm calculated that its investment of $3 million was fully recovered in the first three years of operation. Table 6-1 shows the figures on which the magazine's judges based their award decision.

TABLE 6-1

Apparent Payoff from the Investment

	Year 1 ($ millions)	Years 2–5 (annual, $ millions)
Costs		
Technology purchases	0.83	0.29
Development/implementation	0.05	0
Maintenance and support	0.02	0.08
Systems operations	0.04	0.11
Total	$0.94	$0.49
Returns		
Reduced operating costs	0.60	1.17
Reduced capital investment	0.14	0.17
Indirect cost avoidance	0.12	0.14
Total	$0.86	$1.47
Net return on investment	$0.09	$0.98

Unfortunately, these figures are incomplete and misleading. Here are a few examples of the relevant cash flows not included:

- The new process and the technology associated with it are a major organizational transformation, but the costs of education and training are ignored. A reliable rule of thumb is that training amounts to 20 percent of an IT project's cost. In this case, 20 percent of the initial capital cost of equipment and development would be about $200,000. That would mean a very modest $500 per employee for the approximately 400 workers in the customer-service claims processing departments.

- Management time, the fees of consultants who played a major role, planning time, and other costs of change are absent. These costs could not have been less than $200,000.

- Indicated technology expenses badly understate the cost of support and administration. As I said earlier, hidden capital costs associated with computer technology dwarf the purchase price of hardware and software. The Gartner Group estimates that it costs $8,000 to $18,000 per year to support each user in a networked environment. A 1992 Ferris Networks survey concluded that a full-time support person is needed for every 40 users. In this case, that would mean ten people at a cost of at least $45,000 per year each. The firm's estimate of $84,000 for maintenance and support is far too low.[2]

- Improved customer service means faster payments. The firm's annual revenues are close to $300 million. If we assume that it pays back 80 percent of this in claims, that amounts to $20 million a month. Just as speeding up the collection of receivables increases available cash, so speeding up payments reduces free capital. Cutting deferred payables by two-thirds (30 days to 10 days) reduces them by just under $14 million, to $6.6 million. I estimate the firm's cost of capital at 18 percent, so the loss of free capital costs $14 million times 18 percent, or $2.5 million per year.

- Approximately 80 workers were laid off. If we assume modest a severance of four weeks' pay on an average salary of $18,000, that adds $112,000, excluding administrative and ancillary costs.

- Reduced capital investment is treated as the same kind of cash flow savings as that in operational expenses. The true savings is the reduced cost of capital, not the total reduction in investment. At 18 percent, that is $25,000 in the first year and $31,000 each year thereafter, not $140,000 and $170,000.

Hidden costs change the whole picture. Taxes also need to be taken into account, of course. Training, support, and anything else the firm can expense has additional value compared to nondeductible items. Similarly, operational savings are reduced by the extra tax incurred. My own plausible estimates of the real expenses associated with the reengineering project show a total capital expenditure that is more than double the firm's estimates (see Table 6-2). Note that the hidden drain on EVA is the very efficiency the innovation created—the "improvement" in paying claims in ten days instead of thirty days. The twenty-day float was, in effect, free capital. I'm not suggesting that it's a good idea to finance your operations at the expense of your customers' satisfaction and bank balance. I'm merely challenging the claims that an annual "return" of $860,000 (first year) and $980,000 (second through fifth years) is real when it costs $2.5 million per year to fund.

TABLE 6-2

THE REAL COSTS OF THE PROCESS INVESTMENT

	YEAR 1 ($ MILLIONS)	YEARS 2–5 (ANNUAL, $ MILLIONS)
Technology purchases	0.83	0.29
Development/implementation	0.05	0
Training	0.20	0.05
Maintenance and support	0.45	0.60
Systems operations	0.04	0.11
Severance	0.11	0
Planning and change management	0.20	0
Capital cost of faster payment	2.52	2.52
Total	$4.40	$3.57

It is clear that the award-winning return on investment is a myth. The project drains rather than generates economic value. This example is not meant to demonstrate that hubbing is likely to be a bad idea for most firms. The health care firm may have realized quantifiable benefits that I have overlooked as well as other important benefits that cannot be quantified. In many instances, hubbing is likely to provide important value that is not measurable as direct financial return. And it may increasingly be an investment that must be made to provide a competitive level of customer service. But firms gain nothing from miscalculating their true costs. Sound process investment decisions must be based on an accurate understanding of the capital they use. This project will contribute to the process paradox of apparent benefit and real loss.

IMPORT: BRING IN PROCESSES FROM OTHER KINDS OF BUSINESS

This strategy builds value by adopting a process developed in another industry when that process is superior to the "local" processes for accomplishing the same basic tasks. Importing rests on management's ability to abandon the kind of traditional thinking discussed in Chapter 3. Narrowly fixed on what it considers core industry processes, traditional thinking is unable to imagine how a firm can benefit from processes associated with radically different kinds of business. The importing value builder does just that.

Rather than compare themselves with their main competitors, firms that are open to importing processes ask, "Who is the very best at handling this process, regardless of what business they happen to be in?" This kind of benchmarking is a proven way to exploit opportunities to import processes. Banc One of Ohio asked what organization was best at marketing in stores, not which bank did the best job. It decided that the clothing retailer Benetton set the standard and used that company's processes as a guide for rethinking the whole subject of bank branches. Xerox decided it could learn most about fulfilling customers' phone orders from L. L. Bean. When IBM wanted to improve its processes for filling orders for small parts that have to be carefully packaged, it looked at Marriott Hotels' airline food service subsidiary, whose expertise in assembling the components of in-flight meals could be applied to cables, batteries, disks, and manuals. Similarly, Southwest Airlines, already the industry leader in efficiently preparing planes for their next flights, took lessons from Indianapolis 500 pit crews to learn how to be even better at turning the planes around.

It is fairly common for companies to find new purposes for their existing processes. British Airways' use of its reservations processes to make hotel reservations for its customers is one example among many. Firms less frequently import new processes to accomplish tasks they are already doing. But finding opportunities to do so becomes more and more important as competition continues to increase and stable, bounded industries become the exception rather than the rule. At a time when AT&T and GM are leaders in credit cards and Ford is as much a financer as a seller of cars, companies need to look outside their traditional core processes to learn the best ways to do things.

Importing a process is usually more efficient than inventing one from scratch. When Maryland adopted ATMs for its electronic benefits services, it profited from the banking industry's extensive investment in the machinery's development while incurring little risk and very moderate costs. The barriers to and risks involved in importing processes derive from the firm's moving beyond its established capabilities to procure a "foreign" process. The imported process is likely to challenge long-standing corporate assumptions. To carry out the process successfully, the company has to build new skills and systems and acquire experience and new management expertise. Although the capital costs of planning and sustained training are easy to overlook and underfund, the imported process may not function well if those activities are neglected.

COLLABORATE: COORDINATE PEOPLE, NOT JUST ACTIVITIES

Collaboration focuses on improving the way people work together to carry out processes rather than on the process activities themselves. It emphasizes teamwork and trust and depends on communication and cooperation. Streamlining coordinates a sequence of activities in which people are generally, though not always, subordinated to the goal of process efficiency. Hubbing may lead to job enrichment by putting an entire process in the hands of an individual, but its primary aim is to coordinate decision and information flows, not to change the way people work together. Collaboration is about people, not work flows. Investment in this process value builder goes toward improving how people share information, negotiate, manage requests and commitments, and work together to meet performance targets.

Collaboration can link processes that have been streamlined, hubbed, or otherwise reengineered, or it can coordinate processes that have not themselves been improved. It is an appropriate strategy to apply to processes or sets of processes that depend on judgment. Unlike the processes described by the Penzias axiom, which can be satisfactorily handled by computers, these processes require people to interact with customers and one another. When processes cannot be reduced to well-defined rules and depend on cooperation, leverage people, don't reengineer the process.

A striking example of the potential of the collaboration value builder comes from Concretos, the ready-mix concrete division of Cemex, one of the world's leading and most aggressive cement companies. Concretos had invested substantial effort and cash in streamlining many of its processes but derived little benefit from the changes. Like many manufacturing firms, the company was organized around its own operational priorities rather than its customers' needs. The processes that most concerned the customer—ordering and delivery—were driven by the manufacturing schedule. The sales force was little more than a group of order takers who mediated between the customers and manufacturing. The firm was a leader in its market, but its prices were higher than those of its competitors, who were increasingly lowering prices to capture market share (although at the cost of their own profitability).

The firm undertook an initiative that it called reengineering, but it was much different from reengineering programs that are essentially staff-reducing and cost-cutting exercises. Concretos instead focused on collaboration as the basis of business processes, defining *process* this way: "Rather than tracking the flow of materials or data, business processes chart the coordination of action between people (and sometimes machines) involved in an activity."[3]

This conception turned the attention of Concretos's management and sales staff to coordination with the customer. Sales representatives spent time learning how to listen to the customer's concerns, rather than just thinking about making the sale. They discovered that the basic and largely unexpressed concern of customers was not price or even quality, but scheduling: they needed to be sure that the concrete would arrive at construction sites at just the right time. If it came too early, they would either have to dump it or urgently reschedule activities. If it came late, they would have to pay workers for idle time. To solve this problem, Concretos did not need to reengineer process steps; it needed a new approach to coordinating existing processes. As the project team modeled the flow of requests, commitments, and actions, they found many unintended breakdowns, gaps, and ambiguities in coordination. For instance, changes in production scheduling that were designed to optimize manufacturing work flows could affect customers without the knowledge of either the production group or the sales force.

Concretos's entire sales and customer-service processes were transformed by beginning with the customer's requirements. The reengineering team worked back from there, identifying the breakdowns in collaboration that prevented well-meaning sales, marketing, and manufacturing personnel from working effectively together. While collaborating to satisfy individual units within the company (such as guaranteeing tidy documentation and conformance to standard operating procedures), they maintain their goal to satisfy the *customer*. Concretos is now using a mix of new people skills developed through training and new software that links people and subprocesses to do business in a new way. Without making major changes in the processes themselves, it has used collaboration to provide a higher level of service for which customers are willing to pay a premium.

WORKNET: EXTENDING COLLABORATION

The term *worknet* was coined by Michael Schrage, a journalist who has written extensively on collaborative work. In his book *No More Teams,* he distinguishes between coordination and collaboration.[4] Coordination, he says, means working together to get a job done. Collaboration means working together to accomplish much more than you can by working alone. Scientific research, some kinds of writing, and other creative activities can benefit from such collaboration. Worknetting is an extension of collaboration. It goes beyond the coordination of people who work on a set of related processes to a wider and more open-ended creative collaboration.

For more than twenty years, Digital Equipment has viewed worknetting as one of the most important contributors to overall productivity. According to DEC's former chairman, Ken Olsen, the ability to coordinate the activities of a worldwide team through telecommunications is essential in an era of time-based competition. The firm identified team-building and communications as priority processes and has made a huge investment in a global communications network that links 85,000 computers.

In 1991, a senior manager commented that DEC had to adapt to a "white water of change. . . . Digital Equipment Corporation faces some of the most difficult challenges the company has faced in its industry. People are dealing daily with complexities never experienced before. . . . The network is the unifier and enabler that enhances Digital's management models and responses."[5] Although DEC's network-based worknet has not overridden the company's many problems, it has generated significant value. DEC directly attributes to worknetting (1) a reduction of materials management planning cycles from as much as 150 days to fewer than 30, (2) a halving of time-to-market and manufacturing cycles, (3) an increase in inventory turnover from 2 to 4.6 times per year, and (4) a savings of $1 billion in operations costs. As DEC says, "The network is the system."

There are internal and external worknets. An internal worknet links the company's employees and locations, with perhaps limited links to outside organizations for handling standard transactions such as purchase orders and payments. Some companies that have made end-to-end logistics a priority asset process have developed external worknets, extending the processes of collaboration, teamwork, and information sharing to suppliers and customers. Wal-Mart, for instance, allows major suppliers like Levi Strauss & Co. to tap directly into its databases to find out how its products are selling and to restock the stores without waiting for purchase orders.

Boeing Co. worknetted the entire development of its 777 aircraft. The company involved customers in the design process and incorporated their insights into the final plans. American Airlines persuaded Boeing to change the fittings for reading lights, and others convinced the company to redesign the galleys, to name only two of the many productive interactions that occurred. Initially, some of Boeing's designers were frustrated by the inclusion of outsiders and the many long meetings and frequent arguments that resulted. Over time, though, a spirit of open collaboration developed. There is now general agreement that the process resulted in a better plane for both Boeing and its customers. Boeing estimated that its worknetted, computer-based design process cut costs and time by 25 percent.

THE TRUST FACTOR

Michael Schrage points out that just providing tools for coordination and communication does not create the climate of trust and cooperation needed for true collaboration.[6] The network is the infrastructure for information sharing, but it only serves that purpose if people are willing to share information. Like the telephone system, it has no value unless people use it for communication. A network is just machinery; a team-based, collaborative culture turns the network into a worknet.

Shoshana Zuboff, author of *In the Age of the Smart Machine,* says that computers have generally been used to automate processes in large organizations.[7] She argues in favor of using them to "informate" rather than automate. When process control systems are installed in manufacturing plants, the staff who operate them can become slaves of the machine, watching dials and following standard procedures while their supervisors give orders and make decisions. But the information available through the system often gives workers a broader and clearer understanding of the work than their supervisors have. If they are allowed and encouraged to use that understanding and take responsibility for the process, they become part of a worknet and create more value for the company than if they function as automatons.

Schrage's and Zuboff's comments suggest the primacy of trust in collaboration and worknetting. Internally, trust is the key to making empowerment real, to breaking down functional boundaries and fiefdoms and encouraging genuine information sharing. Trust must exist among employees and between management and employees if genuine collaboration is to take place. Trust is as much a skill as a value, having to do not just with honesty but with reliability and competence. External worknets depend on what we might call "tough trust." Retailers such as Dillard and Wal-Mart set very demanding high standards for their suppliers but, in return, work closely with them. They avoid surprises and playing vendors off against one another, aiming for long-term, stable relationships rather than short-term advantages. Texas Instruments similarly worknets with its suppliers via its global telecommunications network, which it also uses for its internal coordination. The company gives its suppliers detailed information on their performance, helps them to troubleshoot and monitor, and meets weekly with them to review joint operation of the network. Texas Instruments holds suppliers to the toughest standards, but treats them as true partners.

DIFFICULT BUT ESSENTIAL

Worknetting is probably the most complex and expensive of my value builders. It involves major capital investment in technology and people and creates many organizational uncertainties and risks. The trust that successful worknetting requires is not easy to build or maintain in relationships that are simultaneously cooperative and competitive. Nevertheless, most expert commentators see worknetting as essential to competing in the economy of today and tomorrow. The processes on which it depends—alliance- and trust-building as much or more than communications and technology—are important assets and will become increasingly so in the future.

LONG-TERM COMMITMENT FOR LONG-TERM VALUE

The process value builders described in this chapter generally require a considerable commitment of time and capital. Enhancing processes entails understanding them in detail, planning changes with care, and often making significant capital investments in equipment, support, and training. Worknetting, as I have said, is likely to be especially complex and costly. Managers often seriously underestimate the costs of such process enhancements as streamlining and hubbing and predict unrealistic short-term savings. Like most other capital investments, process enhancements usually generate value over time. They are not quick fixes. Several years may pass before the value they create for the firm equals the cost of the capital invested in them, but successful process enhancements can provide lasting value. They may not bolster next month's revenues, but they can contribute to the firm's future economic health.

CHAPTER 7

PROCESS VALUE BUILDERS

BASIC CHANGE

MY FINAL CATEGORY OF VALUE BUILDERS INCLUDES THOSE THAT result in basic changes in processes and, often, in the way the organization views itself and is seen by customers and investors. These revolutionary value builders are likely to bring with them considerable risk, but they promise the greatest payoff and most sustained competitive advantage when successful. Business process investment of this kind takes the organization beyond the improvement and enhancement of existing processes into new territory.

Not all revolutionary value builders involve high risk. Firms that take a creative approach to looking for a process edge may discover or invent processes that open new avenues of opportunity without massive capital investment or abandoning currently successful ways of doing business. Many of these low-risk opportunities (and some of the high-risk ones) have been created by deregulation and developments in information technology. I've touched on the fact that deregulation has removed traditional boundaries between industries. At the same time, telecommunications and computer technology have erased many of the barriers of time and distance that once prevented companies from entering certain markets or providing certain services. As a result of these developments, firms that think in terms of potential new applications of existing processes have opportunities to develop entirely new sources of corporate value. In some cases, they may turn current processes into new products, or "productize" a process; in others, they may use their processes to capture someone else's customers—what I call "preempting." These strategies, along with franchising, radicalizing, and inventing, are revolutionary process value builders.

PRODUCTIZE: TURN A PROCESS INTO A PRODUCT

When MCI introduced its "Friends and Family" service, it turned a set of background liability processes into a product. Its accounting and billing processes became the basis for a customized discount service that generated $2 billion per year for the company. MCI's success at productizing a process resulted from two factors. One was the company's creativity—its recognition that processes that are usually considered necessary but unexceptional could be turned into an exciting new product. The other was the fact that MCI handled these processes differently from AT&T, its main competitor, in a way that made it technically difficult for that company to duplicate the program.[1] A process difference—a superiority in terms of its ability to track calls—was turned into a product advantage.

Productizing can be seen as the obverse of importing a process. Rather than adopting another company's superior process for accomplishing a necessary existing task, a firm finds a new use for a process that it already handles especially well. A company whose primary business is handling telephone orders for flowers turned its background credit card authorization and payment processes into a product that it sells to small companies who need that capability but cannot afford the infrastructure and staff required. A typical customer might be a small bookstore that gains the ability to take credit card orders over the phone without having to become a Visa or MasterCard merchant, a status that entails paperwork and deferred payments.

Turning a process into a product can create significant EVA if it is done without massive new capital investment. When it uses an existing process in a new way, a firm generates revenue from investment it has already made. It can sell the process-based service for less than it would cost a buyer to replicate it. American Express and several other leading travel agent chains sell travel management services to large companies that would otherwise need to commit substantial capital to building internal travel agencies, including the cost of developing the expertise that American Express and other established agencies have built up over the years.

In all of these examples, firms successfully turned processes into products because they handled those processes with unusual skill and efficiency or because it was not practical for other firms to match their significant capital investment in comparable internal processes. Often both reasons apply. When Federal Express created its Business Logistics subsidiary, it counted on the fact that most other firms could not duplicate its skill at delivering and tracking small packages *and* on the knowledge of what it would cost another company to develop its own infrastructure to provide the service that Business Logistics offered.

Because turning a process into a product involves creative insight, there are no specific rules for productizing. These general approaches, however, may be helpful in seeking opportunities to productize: look at processes currently hidden from customers that could benefit them if directly offered as a product or service; look at other industries to identify processes that you have and that they either lack or execute much less efficiently than you do.

FRANCHISE: LICENSE PROCESSES, INFRASTRUCTURE, AND EXPERTISE

McDonald's, H&R Block, Mrs. Field's Cookies, and many other firms franchise their process expertise. Franchisees generally pay for a combination of procedures, software services, and training. In addition, and equally important, they buy the use of the franchiser's name, which customers value as a guarantee of an expected product quality or level of service.

Franchisees get the benefit of the McDonald's reputation for quality and consistency—a reputation that persists because that company has defined and standardized its key processes rigorously and transfers them successfully to the entrepreneurs who own individual restaurants. Those entrepreneurs buy a complete set of process capabilities, not an off-the-shelf product. McDonald's provides the oversight and training, as well as the food distribution infrastructure, to make sure that its standards are upheld.

Franchising a process is much different from franchising a facility. Several hotel chains that allowed individual owners to use their names in return for a franchising fee debased the value of those names by not ensuring the quality of check-in, cleaning, décor, food, and other services. In 1992, a major hotel franchiser was forced to eliminate more than 20 percent of its hotels because they did not meet minimally acceptable standards. The damage done to a well-known name can be a lasting problem. What stays in the mind of a dissatisfied customer is not that he or she stayed at one poor hotel but that XYZ Hotels are poor in general. The franchise name becomes as much of a liability as the McDonald's name is an asset.

Identify asset processes that can create a new business for someone else when transferred along with corresponding infrastructures and expertise. Such opportunities are relatively rare. Realizing them requires outstanding definition, process packaging, and management of the transfer process; the rewards, however, can be substantial. In return for the use of their names and process capabilities, McDonald's and H&R Block receive substantial license fees; franchisees bear the cost of real estate.

RADICALIZE: RAISE THE ORGANIZATIONAL STAKES

Radicalizing a process means deliberately raising its salience. Radicalizing does not in and of itself alter the process; it establishes new corporate priorities and makes it clear that the radicalized process and the processes that support it have management attention and backing. When Ford made quality "Job 1," its aim was to turn quality into an identity asset. It radicalized the processes on which quality depends and made their improvement a top priority. Radicalizing does not specify how processes should be changed: the people who analyze a process to determine what value builder should be applied to it may make the same choice whether the process has been radicalized or not. Still, the leadership implicit in radicalizing is itself a value builder.

A key point made by reengineering theorists is that the solid support of senior management is required for successful change. These people's commitment to change matters more than the details of the plan for change. In part, that commitment means being willing to make the investments of time and capital that change requires, but it also means guiding the firm through the complexities and uncertainties of change. Change is difficult. Some process movement proponents ascribe the failure of some reengineering projects to "resistance to reengineering" and seem at a loss to understand why people would resist clear improvements in work processes. Shoshana Zuboff suggests that reengineering appeals to computer professionals because they think it does not involve dealing with people.[2] But change is about people, not engineering diagrams. In *Managing on the Edge,* Richard Pascale analyzes what happened at Ford when management radicalized quality processes. He shows that the company's transformation was not a tidy, rational process but a situation rife with conflict and uncertainty—a situation ameliorated by the vision, values, and commitment (and sometimes the luck) of senior management.[3]

Radicalize processes when the actions and commitment of people are more important drivers of positive change than specific process activity reforms. Radicalizing is most appropriately applied to complex, important sets of processes rather than, say, a single background or priority process. It is a means by which senior management offers a broad vision that directs those who administer the details of process change.

PREEMPT: USE YOUR PROCESS TO CAPTURE SOMEONE ELSE'S CUSTOMER

Discussing the problem of traditional thinking in Chapter 3, I described firms that successfully used preempting to capture customers who "belong" to another industry. British Airways was able to enter the hotel reservations business profitably because

1. It already had a computerized reservations system that cost nearly $500 million to build, an amount that created a barrier to entry for other firms.

2. It had access to customers at a key moment of value—when they booked their flights and would be needing a hotel room. (The airline's agents would have had little success trying to sell customers VCRs.)

3. It had predatory instincts—both the *will* to move aggressively into a business area occupied by another industry and the *insight* to see an opportunity outside its core activities.

Similarly, McKesson, a supplier to pharmacies, used its existing relationship with pharmacies and its electronic data handling infrastructure to become the fourth-largest insurance claims processor in the United States. By providing convenient and reliable handling of what would have been a cumbersome administrative process, it preempted the health insurance industry and, in 1992, was selected to handle the entire industry's electronic claims processing services. McKesson's move into claims process is an example of both preempting and productizing—turning its own data management processes into a service it could sell to pharmacists and insurance firms.

Appropriate infrastructure and timely access to customers are necessary conditions of successful preempting; reputation can also be important if that identity asset contributes to the customer's willingness to purchase a new product or service. Tesco, the British supermarket chain, provides an example. The firm is among the world's top supermarkets in terms of business excellence. Its original identity processes related to pricing. Its founder, as influential in British retailing as Sam Walton has been in the United States, made his firm one of the largest supermarket chains in Britain on the "pile 'em high and sell 'em low" principle. Tesco has matured into a company known both for aggressive pricing and consistent quality, with strong house brands. When it set up forecourt service stations to supply gas to motorists under the Tesco brand name (although obviously the product comes from oil companies such as Texaco), it captured 20 percent of the United Kingdom's gas market in just two years. The venture succeeded because it offered a product at a potential moment of value—customers were already driving to a Tesco store to buy groceries—and because the company's reputation for quality and price convinced motorists that Tesco gas would be a good deal.

Marks and Spenser, another British retailer, used its expertise in managing fast-moving consumer goods and its reputation for quality to enter the business of selling perishable foods. In 1995, its Paris store was *the* place to go for take-out lunches. According to the *Economist,* Marks and Spenser was the most profitable retailer in the world in that year.[4]

Look at your customer's moment of value and consider where you can capture new business through your existing process infrastructures. And remember, your customer does not care about industry boundaries; all he or she wants is service and convenience. Customers make hotel reservations through British Airways because that is a convenient and reliable way to secure a hotel room; they are not influenced by the thought that it might be more "appropriate" to use the hotel's reservations service instead. Tesco's success as a gasoline retailer also shows that the distribution channel can be a more important "brand" than the name on the product. Consumers respond to Tesco's reputation and the convenience of buying gas at its stores; they don't care whether the gas came from Texaco's refineries or Shell's.

As the boundaries between industries continue to dissolve, preemption will become an increasingly important process investment strategy. Over the next few years, we can expect to see Fidelity Investments more and more preempting financial service providers, Wal-Mart preempting supermarkets and other retailers (as it is already doing with its Sam's Club stores), and Citibank preempting travel services (Citibank already has its own Citibank phone-based travel agency). In developing its process investment strategy, a firm needs both to look at its future preempting opportunities and to be prepared for the likelihood that other companies will try to preempt some of *its* current business.

INVENT: BUILD A NEW PROCESS, DON'T REBUILD AN OLD ONE

The firm that invents a new process can sometimes enjoy a significant and long-lasting competitive advantage. Studies of innovative airline reservations systems, developments in retailing logistics, just-in-time manufacturing, and new ways of marketing financial services show that a process invention can keep competitors at bay for seven to ten years. A successful new major business process usually relies on investments in training, collaboration, and technology and cannot therefore be easily or quickly duplicated. In some cases, however, duplicating another firm's innovation at a lower cost than the pioneer's still does not outweigh the disadvantage of entering a business area years behind the leader.

Process inventions can and usually do build on existing processes. Ned Johnson of Fidelity Investments used familiar direct marketing and telemarketing processes to create a new kind of investment service in an environment that had depended on branch offices and customer account managers. Michael Dell's innovation was to apply existing mail-order and package-delivery services to Dell's computer retailing. He did not have to invent package delivery; he used UPS.

Sometimes the concepts underlying process invention are relatively simple. Some straightforward but valuable new processes have been developed to address existing business problems. USA Truck invented a process to deal with a problem endemic to the trucking industry. Trucking typically has an extremely high turnover rate. Because the work is brutally hard and drivers often spend two to four weeks continuously on the road, an annual 100 percent or even 200 percent attrition rate is not uncommon. It costs at least $3,000 to recruit and train a new driver. Figure in lost business and lower productivity, and the real cost of replacing a driver is closer to $12,000.

USA Truck found a way to cut its turnover rate from 105 percent to 85 percent. In one year it saved $500,000 in recruiting and training alone, a substantial addition to its earnings of $5.6 million. Its expense ratio is 87 percent, compared with an industry average of 95 percent. Its stock price rose 50 percent between 1992 and 1994. These gains resulted from USA Truck's invention of a process that can be called "driver care." According to *Forbes*, USA Truck devised "a unique way to handle the shortage of long-haul truck drivers. Be nice to the drivers."[5] The company has developed communications links to help stranded drivers get back on the road quickly. It installed private showers instead of communal bathrooms at its main terminal drivers' dormitory. It has new drivers ride with experienced ones on their first trips; it gives them reduced mileage quotes and does not require them to drive to difficult destinations such as Boston until they have gained experience. USA Truck's driver care processes benefit the drivers and the company. In return for the support it gives drivers, the company demands on-time deliveries from them: a driver who is late twice a year is fired. Unlike firms that guarantee delivery to the day, USA Truck guarantees it to the hour, and charges customers who need that level of precision a 3 percent premium.

Many financial services firms have developed new processes to solve a problem when they realized that their focus on attracting new customers was a drain on corporate value. The experience of Chemical Banking Corp. is representative. In 1993, Chemical launched a marketing campaign to attract students, offering special rates. The campaign was a success in that 20,000 new customers signed up, but it usually takes 3 to 5 years for an account to become profitable, so the firm's success really meant an economic loss. Chemical and other financial institutions (along with magazines, whose new-subscriber incentives encouraged existing subscribers to let their subscriptions lapse so that they could resubscribe at lower rates) invented new processes to retain customers. Some customer-retention processes are as simple as keeping names and addresses updated and following up with customers whose accounts have become inactive; others involve cross-selling and improving customer relations. These new processes have the potential to generate substantial value. In financial services, increasing customer retention by 5 percent per year increases total operating margins by 95 percent.

Some of the more radical proponents of reengineering have argued that a fresh start is a necessity. They see American business in such terrible shape that the only option is to throw away the old structures and invent new ones. I see process invention as one option among many—a powerful choice when appropriate, but by no means the only one.

VALUE BUILDERS: CHOICE AND FLEXIBILITY

The process value builders I have described in this and the previous two chapters offer managers a range of opportunities and options. There is no single solution to every business process problem or a single strategy that is, by nature, superior to all others. The appropriateness of a particular value builder depends on the kind of process to which it is applied, the nature of the corporate environment, and the wider business environment. Using a particular value builder can create opportunities to use others. Hubbing, for instance, may lead to process improvements that make it possible to productize a service that had been a background liability. Radicalizing a process can improve the success possibilities of a range of other value builders. Some process investment may simultaneously involve two value builders, as when a process is both productized and preempts another firm's business. Managers who examine their firms' process portfolios for investment opportunity are likely to use several kinds and combinations of value builders. A flexible approach and a variety of choices provide the best means of generating new economic value through process investment.

CHAPTER 8

BUILDING AN ENTERPRISE STRATEGY

LEADERSHIP AND CHANGE

ONE OF THIS BOOK'S PRIMARY THEMES IS THAT BUSINESS PROCESS investment cannot be successfully carried out in a vacuum. Much of my focus has been on what can be considered external factors that affect process investment decisions: competitive pressures, customer expectations, technological developments and regulatory changes that create new opportunities or change the rules of competition, and shareholder valuation. In this chapter I look at the ways in which the character of the firm influences what processes are targeted for investment and what kind of investment is made in them. Culture, structure, and style strongly affect the kinds of process changes a company will attempt and the kinds it is likely to carry out successfully.

My examination here is more descriptive than prescriptive. I delineate the ways in which different firms deal with process change so that managers will be able to recognize some of the factors driving (or impeding) change in their organizations and evaluate their own and their companies' ways of handling process investment.

LEVELS OF COMMITMENT TO CHANGE

A firm looking for process investment opportunities is likely to apply a variety of value builders to its portfolio of processes. Not all of those value builders will carry exactly the same risk and involve the same degree of change, but firms tend to focus their efforts on a particular level of change. Leadership, culture, organizational confidence, and expectations, which I call "change drivers," collectively define the degree of a firm's commitment to change. Change drivers are related to but different from strategic styles, which I discuss later in the chapter. I can organize the range of commitment to change in four basic categories: incremental, step-shift, radical, and fundamental. Parallels exist between these levels of commitment and my organization of value builders on a scale ranging from low-risk process adjustments to revolutionary process change and invention. I think, though, that these categories, each of which may involve applying several kinds of value builders, provide a useful framework for understanding what companies do in practice.

INCREMENTAL CHANGE

With incremental change, management is committed to moving forward in deliberate and phased steps. This kind of change is not necessarily cautious or without risk: taking incremental steps along a tightrope can be challenging. The value builders most associated with incremental change are streamlining and relatively low-risk adjustments such as outsourcing, self-sourcing, and abandoning.

Many managers today tend to treat incremental change as always necessarily inadequate. A continuously changing and increasingly competitive business environment does in fact often require more than incremental improvement, even in firms that have been successful for decades by performing familiar tasks in familiar ways. Recall the words of Paul O'Neil, the chairman of

Alcoa: "Continuous improvement is exactly the right idea if you are the world leader in everything you do. It is a terrible idea if you are lagging in the world leadership benchmark."[1] But there are situations in which incrementalism is the best choice, at least for a time.

Some companies thrive on incremental improvement because they come close to meeting O'Neil's requirement: they are leaders in the activities that count most. McDonald's, for instance, has for the most part maintained its enviable position by making incremental improvements in processes that were already superior to those of its competitors. A radical change in a system that works so well would not make sense. Firms in environments that have remained relatively stable amid the instability of the global economy are also likely to do well with incremental change.

I have, however, described the danger of believing that an environment is stable when it is not and being caught unawares by a rival who has changed the rules of competition. Sears ignored the challenge from Wal-Mart and assumed that gradual improvements in its retailing processes would ensure continued success. It wasted its efforts on incremental change (and in some areas made no change at all) when more dramatic shifts were required. Even McDonald's has occasionally had to employ more than incremental improvements to respond to external changes. In the early 1990s, for example, the company found that shifting demographics and consumer habits were reducing the profitability of many of the large restaurants that were the core of its business. In 1991, average revenue per restaurant fell for the first time ever. Although productivity and earnings remained high, McDonald's rate of growth slowed, and the pressure on margins increased. Investors recognized the worrisome trend, and the price-to-earnings ratio of the firm's stock dropped. McDonald's responded by inventing new, mid-size and small restaurants and developing new franchising agreements and operating procedures appropriate to them—a strategy that seems to have been successful.

Although even the most successful and stable firms should be alert to pressures and challenges that must be met with innovative change, it would be wrong to ignore the value of incrementalism as a strategy for change and process investment. McDonald's development of new processes occurred in the context of ongoing successful incrementalism. Firms such as J. P. Morgan & Co. and Home Depot rarely attract headlines because their continued success is based on sustained improvement, not dramatic change.

STEP-SHIFT CHANGE

With step-shift change, top management is committed to shifting gears, making significant process changes but not changing the basic direction of the business and how it generates value. Step-shift change typically focuses on applying value builders such as hubbing, preempting, and worknetting to a portfolio of priority processes.

Microsoft Corp. is a firm that generally relies on step-shifting to maintain its dominant position. It goes beyond incrementalism, generating a flood of new products while improving existing ones, but in the context of a consistent, focused strategy. Because Microsoft effectively dominates the computer operating system and office software environment, its moderate changes often force competitors into more radical and risky strategies that they hope will give them some advantage over the giant. Even Microsoft, though, is not immune to challenges from outside. The explosive growth of the Internet and the success of Netscape in creating Internet software that may eventually make parts of today's operating systems obsolete have caused Microsoft to transfer significant resources to developing Internet products. Rather than set the pace in this area, Microsoft has had to respond to the pacesetter and change the focus of its efforts very quickly.

Some firms whose leadership and culture have been most comfortable with incremental change are driven to step-shift change by environmental factors. Glaxo, the pharmaceuticals firm, has a long history of success based on the strength of its research and its aggressive marketing. The latter helped make the antiulcer drug Zantac the industry's first billion-dollar-a-year product. Wide-ranging pressures for health care reform in the United States, cost-cutting by European government health agencies, and tightened cost control by insurers and health maintenance organizations have combined to increase the importance of pricing and the manufacture of less-expensive generic drugs—weak areas for Glaxo. The company has had to resort to step-shift change in response, an adjustment that it has not found easy. Glaxo's chief executive officer, Ernest Mario, resigned in 1993 because he disagreed with the firm's decision to strengthen the marketing of generics; Chairman Paul Girolami, who had been the driving force behind Zantac and the company's extensive commitment to research, saw the shift to generics as literally threatening Glaxo's identity.

RADICAL CHANGE

With radical change, management commits to aggressive actions that leave the existing business entity and its basic assumptions intact. The identity of the firm is not in question, but the way it carries out business may be significantly altered. Radicalizing, collaborating, importing, and franchising are some of the value builders that may be employed.

Lou Gerstner's leadership at IBM is an example of a commitment to radical change. Rather than rebuilding the troubled firm from the ground up, Gerstner has developed new asset processes and repaired liability processes while preserving IBM's identity. Although early critics faulted Gerstner for not having the vision to make more fundamental changes (including breaking the firm into smaller companies), his strategy seems to have succeeded. Ford management's decision to radicalize quality by making it "Job 1" is another example of commitment to far-reaching change that dramatically alters the way a firm does its work but does not turn it into a different company.

Commitment to radical change is sometimes driven by outside events—IBM is an example, with the company hiring a new, change-oriented CEO to help reverse its decline—and sometimes by existing leadership and culture. A senior executive at British Airways told me that, faced with a choice between alternatives, the firm will choose the more radical because it wants to lead new competitive trends, not follow them.

FUNDAMENTAL CHANGE

With fundamental change, management is committed to creating what will in effect be a new company. Processes, structure, markets, strategy, and even identity are up for review. Preempting, productizing, and invention are likely to be among the value builders used. The risk and potential rewards of fundamental change are high.

Jack Welch, the chairman of General Electric Co., is committed to fundamental change, developing a new vision and structure for the company. He has emphasized that this will take ten to twenty years of sustained commitment. He's bet the company.

LEADERSHIP AND MANAGEMENT STYLES

As in every area of organizational innovation, leadership in business process investment, not delegation, is as vital as the specific value builders in most instances. The commitment of managers to process change and their willingness to invest time and capital— and prestige—in process value builders is essential for success. Often, though not always, management provides a necessary unifying vision for large-scale change. My own review of the process work done in a number of companies reveals a variety of what I call "strategic styles." Strategic style is not strategy but an approach to strategy: it is defined by the role of a firm's leaders and the locus of responsibility; the firm's relative reliance on individuals, teams, and consultants; the ways it handles planning and implementation; and other cultural factors that affect how things get done. No one style is the "right" one; nor is there a simple correspondence between strategic style and the kind of process work a firm undertakes, although some styles are more likely than others to be associated with more or less radical change. A firm's strategic style has to be explicitly considered when developing and implementing a strategy for business process investment. Each style has a distinctive influence on how firms decide which processes to get right and how to improve them. I identify six strategic styles.

TRANSFORMATIONAL LEADERSHIP

In firms characterized by transformational leadership, the personal credibility, commitment, and energy of the CEO drive change. He or she mobilizes the entire firm, embodying a vision that inspires and organizes its activities. Xerox, Ford, British Airways, General Electric and Motorola, Inc., have had this kind of leadership. The first three firms were rescued from deep trouble by leaders who envisioned and articulated new strategic goals and focused the efforts of employees at all levels on achieving them. Motorola has avoided crisis (until recently—it now faces major threats in its cellular phone business) because its leaders anticipated the need for change and vigorously pursued a program to achieve it. General Electric was a sleeping giant when Jack Welch became chairman. By 1994, he had turned the firm into the second most profitable in the United States and the one with the highest market value.

Transformational leadership almost always uses education to mobilize the organization and provide a shared language of change. Educational programs are not designed to build skills—that is the goal of training—as much as to get everyone on the same wavelength and unify efforts. The turnaround at British Airways relied heavily on a program called "Putting Customers First." Senior executives routinely taught sessions in the program, their participation evidence of a commitment to change at the highest levels. Putting Customers First provided common terms and concepts that reshaped attitudes, expectations, and actions; it helped to create a new corporate culture.

Creating a culture that understands its common goal and has a shared vocabulary for describing that goal is an important part of what makes this strategic style work. The leader's vision is often embodied in a slogan or rallying cry that helps maintain the firm's focus. Motorola's "Six Sigma Quality," Ford's "Quality Is Job 1," and British Airways' "The World's Favorite Airline" (along with "Putting Customers First") are all succinct descriptions of what those companies are striving to achieve.

Transformational leadership takes a special kind of boss. The CEOs who succeed at it are remembered as heroes and heroines. Lee Iacocca is famous for rescuing Chrysler, although few remember the details of his strategy, not to mention his mistakes and the essential contributions of many other managers in the firm. Iacocca and some other leaders are flamboyant, but flamboyance is not what transformational leadership is basically about. It is in no way a criticism of Donald Petersen of Ford, Paul Allaire of Xerox, and Colin Marshall of British Airways to say that they are not exciting people. What mobilized their organizations was not charisma but a deep personal commitment that they turned into an organizational value. Because there is no quick and easy way to transform an entire business, fundamental change requires at least a decade of consistent and determined leadership. Vision, commitment, and persistence count more than star quality.

Transformational leadership provides a clear message about where process investments should be made. The people at the top are personally involved in the details of the change program. Although the portfolio of process targets and value builders is likely to be fairly small, each project will be a major one, involving significant investment and change. The risks tend to be high. If the leader's vision and corresponding choice of process investments are flawed, the firm is in trouble; if he or she is a visionary in the best sense of the word, the process payoff can be tremendous.

DELEGATED MANDATE

At least one-third of large organizations have a strategic style that I call "delegated mandate." Leadership sends clear commands down through the organization about the need for change. The targets they identify are usually fairly broad goals like customer service, quality, collaboration and team-building, cost-cutting, and global expansion. Management commitment to change is unambiguously communicated, but the plan for change is generated at lower levels in the organization. The CEO creates a mandate for change, but he or she delegates the task of making it happen to others. Unlike the transformational leader whose vision defines the firm's new direction and who often gets involved in the details of change, he or she typically launches the change campaign but expects the generals and foot soldiers to take the initiative in designing and carrying out the actual program. The kind of change associated with a delegated mandate style most often falls between fundamental change (which turns the organization upside down and can seldom be delegated) and incrementalism (which generally means business as usual but ever better than today's level of performance and does not call for a mandate for basic change). The focus is usually on radical or step-shift change, with reengineering the most common approach.

The leader's call for change is perceived by business units as a mandate for proposing major process investments. Typically, the units set up teams to search for opportunities, making extensive use of consulting firms to help them organize their efforts. At best, a delegated mandate strategic style offers a combination of top-down direction and bottom-up innovation and energy. It encourages exploration and can create new, collaborative, cross-functional teams that generate new ideas. The potential weakness of this style is that it cannot ensure a coordinated approach to process investment. Whereas transformational leadership provides a common vision that it instills in employees at all levels, a delegated mandate style may result in an assortment of largely ad hoc ventures.

Even when these ventures are handled well and do generate value, they are unlikely to add up to much real innovation. When word comes down from the boss to "Do something—Now!" managers are likely to start with obvious targets such as improving customer service, quality, and the efficiency of work flows that relate to customer satisfaction. They are unlikely to look at or have the opportunity to leverage identity and priority asset processes or to apply value builders such as preempting or inventing processes. "Soft" organizational processes such as management decision processes, acquisition processes, and international financing processes are also unlikely to be part of the process investment portfolio.

My own experience with two large Mexican firms illustrates some of the issues associated with the delegated mandate style.[2] The North American Free Trade Agreement (NAFTA) changed the business environment for Mexican companies, putting them in competition with the best U.S. and Asian firms in an open market. Mexico has demonstrated its ability to compete head-to-head with the rest of the world. A global study of automaker productivity in the early 1990s identified General Motors' plant in Hermasillo, Mexico, as the second most productive plant in the world. (The first was the Mercedes-Benz operation in Frankfurt.) Like North American firms, Mexican companies including the two I worked with, are looking for a process edge over their competitors.

The top managers of both firms made it clear to their subordinates that improvements in businesses processes were an imperative. In other words, they created a mandate for change. Firm A is the more aggressive of the two, with a charismatic leader known for his skill in handling acquisition processes. Firm B is more cautious, with significant authority residing in individual business unit managers who feel they have been empowered to run their parts of the company with considerable independence. In both cases, though, top management made change a company priority and delegated the planning and carrying out of change to others.

Although the firms are quite different, they responded to the mandates from their leaders in much the same way. They set up teams to look for process improvement targets; they contacted a number of consulting firms, each of which offered its own reengineering methodology. These proprietary methodologies were all work-flow–based and involved major start-up costs for analyzing existing processes in detail. Most focused on cost-cutting, primarily through staff reduction. Without exception, they addressed only background liability processes.

Both companies experienced mixed results. Some units successfully streamlined administrative processes. Several of the reengineering projects in each firm got badly bogged down. The change teams had begun with enthusiasm and high expectations but had little to show for their efforts after six months and tended to lose sight of just what it was the reengineering was supposed to accomplish. In Firm A, three of six consulting firms, all well-known leaders in reengineering, were fired. (Two of them were rehired by another part of the company to complete another fired firm's project.) In Firm B, several projects fizzled rather than failed, being in effect abandoned at the end of their first phases.

After three years, reengineering had generated some benefits, but far fewer than promised. Several reengineering initiatives directed at customer service succeeded because they were the first systematic efforts ever made to remove obvious waste and superfluous steps from the processes. Not surprisingly, the most successful projects in both firms were TQM programs for manufacturing: increased quality and efficiency in manufacturing are clearly essential in the open competitive arena created by the passage of NAFTA.

The most successful single initiative contrasted strongly with the others. The strategic style in operation was a combination of the company chairman's delegated mandate and the business unit head's commitment to transformational leadership in his own mini-company. The unit head was part of a change team of forty people from all levels. The process they selected was customer service; collaboration was the process builder they chose to apply to it. Because the transformational leader was forced to examine his fundamental beliefs and modes of management, he was "reengineered" along with the process. His business unit and his leadership have been successfully transformed.

Although the teams in both firms enjoyed the opportunity to create their own priorities and direction, they came to wish that top management had provided clearer guidelines for change and had taken a more active role in the process. Without an overarching vision of change provided by the companies' leaders, they concentrated their efforts on the most obvious local process targets. Their limited focus was abetted by reengineering consulting firms that tended not to look beyond the work flows that they were experienced in streamlining. Even though Firm A began with a mandate for more aggressive change than Firm B, their choice of targets and change strategies were very similar, as were their results.

The experience of these Mexican firms is similar to that of North American and European firms that follow the delegated mandate model of change management. This strategic style gives a green light for change but often does not say enough about which way to go.

REACTIVE URGENCY

Reactive urgency is crisis-driven; it is a response—often a late one—to explicit competitive pressures and shifts in the business environment. It is by far the most common strategic style. Almost invariably, reengineering, downsizing, and cost-cutting are the actions taken, usually in customer service or a comparable area in need of urgent attention. The focus is on liability processes, with fast results the goal. The initiative is usually led by a commissar for change—a senior executive with a reputation for toughness.

The response of Tambrands to a business crisis in the early 1990s provides an example of reactive urgency in action. The manufacturer of Tampax tampons was rapidly losing market share, and its diversification efforts were not succeeding. A new management team was brought in. The CEO slashed costs in the first six months, canceled a number of diversification initiatives, and ordered aggressive reengineering and TQM, mainly of engineering, research and design, and information technology processes. His goal was to refocus the company on its established business and brands. As an aggressive response to a recognized crisis, reactive urgency gets the attention of the whole firm and focuses its efforts. It often marches under the banner of a rallying cry. Tambrands instituted an education program for all its managers to teach "a religion of best practices" and instill the principles of TQM.

The urgency of this strategic style makes things happen. It encourages the formation of cross-functional teams driven by the survival instinct. Tambrands set up on-site "lead teams" in every country in which it has a presence. Urgency also creates new opportunities and increases credibility for the information systems (IS) unit, which often takes the lead in reengineering and plays an important role in cross-functional teaming. The chief financial officer of Tambrands remarked that what had historically been a low-level department "is now embedded in the fiber of the business. There's been a real upgrading of status for IS. The sense now is that you can't do anything without them."[3] A business crisis, reengineering, and information technology often go together. The reengineering movement provides legitimacy and a framework for an important IS role. The desire to fix things fast allows IS, a technical function, to make suggestions about business. Most processes with clearly visible work flows—the targets of reactive urgency—depend heavily on IT, and the likely value builders employed—streamlining, hubbing, and worknetting—have a major IT component.

Whether they settle on TQM or reengineering as their approach, firms driven by reactive urgency almost invariably risk the process paradox. Teams usually base their work on a benefits model, not EVA. Called on to fix what's wrong as quickly as possible, they invest effort and cash mainly in background liabilities and ignore identity and priority processes. Tambrands' explicit goal was to "streamline and standardize operations and technology across the board." Its many projects include standardizing financial reporting and performance measures; improving customer order entry; establishing an international communications network; reengineering computer systems; and increasing the efficiency of scrap/reject reporting, purchasing, and finished-goods inventory processes. Tambrands expects dramatic benefits from these initiatives. Certainly reengineering may enable the company to become a low-cost producer, an important change given that much of its lost market share resulted from price hikes. But the company's list of targets is not really a process investment portfolio. It ignores almost entirely the issue of identity processes, although Tambrands is essentially a single-product firm, and the Tampax name is as generic and well-known as Xerox, IBM, and McDonald's. It lost market share to process-smart competitors like Playtex and needs to leverage and protect its identity assets. One financial analyst, expressing skepticism about Tambrands' reengineering efforts, said that the company needs to focus on securing new markets and regaining ground in existing ones, adding that "it's a very, very tough market that they're in, and it's difficult to achieve significant product differentiation."[4]

I have worked as an advisor to and observer of many well-known firms whose strategic style is reactive urgency. Anticipating and heading off problems is preferable to reacting to them—that's when firms often call in consultants like myself to provide a perspective on a situation that they are far more qualified to address but have lost control of. Reaction means defensiveness, and urgency can mean panic. But reactive urgency can still produce value, especially when its bottom-up, team-based focus on fixing things is complemented by a top-down understanding of salience, worth, and EVA. A sense of crisis in combination with the limited point of view of orthodox reengineering can lead to effort and cash wasted on fixing the wrong processes. Applying the principles of salience and worth to evaluate processes can help firms craft a measured response to the challenges that face it rather than just react to a crisis. Reactive urgency is crisis management. It shouldn't preclude cool analysis of which part of the crisis to deal with.

INDIVIDUAL INITIATIVE

Many well-run firms, particularly decentralized ones, rely on individual initiative to institute process change. They expect individual business and IS leaders to discover opportunities for change and set programs in motion. The initiatives often are based on a particular process movement and the work of a process guru. An executive may, for instance, attend a seminar on the learning organization or read Peter Senge's book on that subject and follow up by bringing Senge or other such experts to the firm, to speak to employees or to act as a consultant. He or she may then sponsor in-house seminars to generate interest in the concepts and build enough support and enthusiasm to launch a process-change program based on them. The leader is an advocate and persuader who generates the momentum needed for action. These initiatives tend to be solution-driven rather than defined by a vision or the need to respond to a crisis. Their operating principle is more "Where can we apply this?" than "How can we solve our problem?"

The success of one project is likely to lead to direct extensions and imitations elsewhere in the business. Because each process movement tends to focus on only a few processes and value builders, individual initiative generally leads to a set of projects that are similar to one another. The learning organization and related team-based concepts will target projects that rest on collaboration, whereas TQM will deal with background processes that have well-defined work flows and inputs and outputs. As a result, individual initiative can produce an excessively narrow portfolio of process investments. Narrowness of focus has the advantage of concentration of effort, though. That and the commitment and intelligence of the initiator (and the disciples he or she may gather) can lead to substantial payoff. This strategic style at Motorola, Xerox, and other firms known for quality management moved those firms from individual programs to critical mass to institutionalization of a philosophy of change. My only caveat is that the strategy too easily overlooks processes that do not fit the particular process idea the initiator adopts and therefore may neglect processes and value builders.

SUSTAINED IMPROVEMENT

This strategic style is characterized by a commitment to continuous improvement. It works best for companies—for instance, Merck & Co., Federal Express, Andersen Consulting, and McDonald's—that have established themselves as the best in their fields. They can afford to rely on incremental improvement to maintain competitiveness, with only occasional needs for more radical innovation.

Although their process improvements rarely make headlines, it would be wrong to assume that these firms rest on their laurels. They tend to be consciously and almost obsessively committed to a daily program of improvement. They understand the value of their identity asset processes and rigorously protect them. They set high performance standards for their priority processes and have a reputation for innovation within the fairly well-defined boundaries of the processes they do best. The sustained improvement strategic style is based on an understanding of the firm's process portfolio—a clear sense of which asset processes matter and deserve investment.

Because these firms are so focused on the capabilities and markets they know best, they sometimes falter when they try to move into a new area. Federal Express's failed Zapmail venture and its inability, despite all of its organizational skill, to bring an acquired British company up to speed are instances of a firm unable to transfer its success to a new business or environment. (The fact that the British firm was unionized made it a poor target for Federal Express's culture and processes.) Wal-Mart had to abandon its effort to create "hypermarkets"—the supermarket-plus-discount-plus-everything stores that are a staple of French retailing. One clear cause of the failure was the fact that Wal-Mart's process expertise did not include an understanding of the temperature-control requirements of huge stores that sell perishable goods.

The best of these firms can survive such lapses. A more serious threat is from shifts in the business environment that are beyond their control but may profoundly affect their business. Merck, which an annual *Fortune* survey rated America's most admired corporation seven years in a row, dropped to eleventh ranking in 1994, when widespread turbulence in the health care field called the continuing success of its long-standing processes into question. In these situations, the best firms respond in one of two ways. They might move from incremental to step-shift change, as McDonald's did when it developed smaller restaurants in response to a drop in revenues at its large ones, or top management may move on to transformational leadership. Although these styles seem very different—one involves vision-led, high-profile change; the other is managed within the existing culture and is often low key—they are related. Almost invariably, transformational leadership builds the outstanding firms that then maintain their primacy with sustained improvement. Sam Walton of Wal-Mart, Ray Kroc of McDonald's, and Fred Smith of Federal Express were all transformational leaders. Faced with a new environmental challenge, these now well-established companies are likely to take the less radical course, but turning the challenge into an opportunity for new fundamental change is also an option. They have the resources, process smarts, and culture to change gear instead of being stuck in the gears they're used to driving in.

OPPORTUNISM

This fairly common style combines willingness to take action when needed to anticipate and prevent crises without stepping too far ahead of competitors. The opportunistic firm is not locked in by its history. It can change when it needs to and generally avoids being pushed into reactive urgency. It is in a good position to exploit the insights and tools offered by process movements, but it generally does not generate distinctive innovations. Such firms do not bet their futures on visions that may or may not work out. They are realists, not idealists.

Opportunism can be a very successful strategy. This safety-first approach to change does limit the kinds of process builders that a firm is likely to employ, however. Inventing, preempting, and other innovative approaches will seem too risky. Also, some opportunistic firms move from one kind of initiative to another, dropping programs that do not generate results fairly quickly in favor of the latest new fashion in management technique. This kind of shifting prevents the firm from getting the benefits of a sustained effort and can reduce management credibility. As one employee of such a firm told me, "Last year it was reengineering. We did TQM in 1993. Every time the boss picks up a book at the airport, we get a new strategy."

A RICH MATRIX OF STYLES AND DRIVERS

As these descriptions and examples show, there are some natural correspondences between strategic styles and change drivers. A sustained improvement style will most often manifest itself in incremental change. Individual initiative is more likely to lead to incremental or step-shift improvements than radical or fundamental change. Transformational leadership, as the phrase suggests, is often associated with a fundamental transformation of the firm. Jack Welch's commitment to realizing his vision of a new General Electric is an obvious example.

The range of correspondences is very broad, however. There are no strict, simple rules that match styles and drivers. Even in companies with the same strategic styles, there is no one right kind of program for change. I've cited the example of McDonald's, a company known for its sustained improvement style, investing in step-shift change when circumstances warranted. Lou Gerstner's transformational leadership at IBM has been directed at radical rather than fundamental change. Percy Barnevik, the head of the giant ABB of Sweden, is as committed to fundamental change as Jack Welch, but his strategic style is most definitely delegated mandate. The factors that govern a firm's choice of process portfolio and value builders are—and should be—complex. In describing the various ways firms invest in change, I am stressing that there are many options, each with its potential risks and rewards. I hope to encourage change managers to broaden their focus and to explore the fullest range of process investment opportunities that they can.

I want to avoid the evangelical, often apocalyptic, tone of guru-ship that hectors managers and instead say, "Good luck to you. Change is tough. You're the managers. Choose the strategy that makes the most sense for you. Choose the style you're most comfortable with."

Clearly, process investment programs will take different forms in different firms—and sometimes different forms in the same firm, when conditions change. In some instances, change is driven from the top and involves a transformation of the firm; in others, it is inspired by managers on the front lines. Some organizational process investments anticipate or even create changes in the business environment; others react to change that originates elsewhere. In all these cases, though, similar structures and procedures can help to make change programs successful. These involve ways of organizing and supervising change to ensure a unified, directed program rather than an ad hoc and possibly self-defeating miscellany of initiatives. These organizing principles are the subject of my next chapter.

CHAPTER 9

BUILDING AN ENTERPRISE STRATEGY

ORGANIZING FOR CHANGE

THE PREVIOUS CHAPTER WAS LARGELY DESCRIPTIVE, SKETCHING various strategic styles and kinds of change and the potential rewards and pitfalls associated with them. In this chapter, I discuss the organizational mechanisms and principles that are essential to successful process investment. My recommendations are modest. I do not propose complex organizational changes or drastic steps. As much as possible, I suggest using well-established and well-understood organizational mechanisms rather than inventing new ones. I recommend

- establishing the right kind of process investment committee to get the right processes right;
- involving long-term planning units in process investment planning;
- developing a common, inclusive language of change;

143

- maintaining a strong and continuing connection among all levels of the firm; and

- providing incentives so that those who implement change benefit from it.

THE PROCESS INVESTMENT CAPITAL COMMITTEE: THE GANG OF X

It is vital to set up a corporate committee to supervise the development and management of the process investment portfolio. The committee's aim, authority, and accountability should be like that of the capital investment planning committees that firms have had for decades. Its mandate is to look after the portfolio, not to micromanage project implementation. It manages capital and monitors, but does not manage delivery. Its goal is to create a perspective and focal point for process investment. Firms that attempt process change without the guidance of such a committee run these related risks:

- There will be no true portfolio, only a set of programs and projects that may or may not add up to the most effective investment opportunities.

- The likely emphasis, established at lower levels of the firm, will be on background liabilities and work flows, rather than on the identity and priority processes that have much more potential to generate value.

- The process paradox—improved processes that fail to make the firm more successful—is almost guaranteed.

I strongly recommend that this committee be organized as a Gang of X, in which "X" is between six and ten people. Among them, these committee members should have the following characteristics, roles, and reputations.

MOVERS

At least four members of the gang should be senior managers who have been explicitly involved in business innovation and are recognized as part of the next generation of business leaders. In the late 1970s, I helped Citibank's international banking division make a radical shift in its use of information technology. The firm established the equivalent of a process investment capital committee and called it the Gang of Eight. One of the eight was the most notorious technophobe among Citibank's top one hundred managers, but he was equally well known as the star innovator of the organization, a brilliant and courageous supporter of his staff in their efforts to invent new ways to succeed in the marketplace. His presence was a clear signal that the decisions that came out of the committee would be acted on. He was hard to persuade, but, once convinced, he made things move. Other gang members were equally driven by the need for action, not just discussion. Movers are essential to the committee both because they make things happen and because they are perceived by others in the firm as making things happen; consequently, they give the process investment plans credibility.

SENIOR LINE MANAGERS

The firm's key business units must be represented by someone with considerable authority, although this does not necessarily have to be the business unit head. Individual business units in large firms may also have their own process investment capital committees. These managers can bring information to the committee about potential process opportunities. Also, their participation in decisions that are likely to affect their business units encourages them and their subordinates to "buy in" to changes that they might resist if they were imposed by a committee external to their part of the firm. Senior line management membership is related to the principle of maintaining connections among all levels of the firm.

THE CHIEF FINANCIAL OFFICER

The firm's CFO or another senior member of corporate finance should be part of the gang to ensure capital financing realism and a focus on EVA. I've observed that the most consistently successful businesses are often quite conservative in their supervision and coordination processes, especially in their management of capital. The CFO is in an ideal position to bring established, traditional financial concerns to bear on often nontraditional approaches to creating a business process edge. He or she is fundamentally a conservator: no matter how radical or even crazy a firm's culture or strategy is, it will not have a radical or crazy CFO.

Tom Peters, the most articulate proponent of the view that old thinking has to go, argues that crazy times demand crazy organizations. I agree, but they do not need crazy spending. Southwest Airlines, whose CEO and founder prides himself on being just a little crazy, returned a 22,000 percent profit to its shareholders between 1975 and 1987. That result reflects disciplined craziness: adventurous marketing and inventive process innovation in a context of economic discipline that kept the firm focused on EVA and therefore market value. Process investment encourages creativity, which is often indistinguishable from craziness, at least until it proves successful. The CFO, or another business manager on the process investment committee, must ensure economic discipline. He or she should evaluate the process portfolio as the manager of a mutual fund would look at his or her portfolio—from the investor's point of view. Does it match the investor's (that is, the firm's) risk profile? Is it unbalanced, with too many projects focused on cutting the costs of background liabilities or, on the other hand, with too many high-cost, high-risk projects? Are the value metrics clear and convincing? That is, will the potential process investments create economic value, enable value to be created, or preserve value?

A HUMAN RESOURCES SENIOR MANAGER

Applying process value builders invariably affects job descriptions, relationships, skill needs, and employment, so human resources needs to have a presence on the committee that instigates process change. A good human resources manager helps keep the committee focused on people, not just on the work flows and technology that many process movements exclusively consider. Human resources can take the lead in developing the incentives that are a key component of an enterprise process investment strategy.

THE DIRECTOR OF INFORMATION SERVICES

Most process value builders involve some investment in IT systems. Hubbing, front-ending, and worknetting require massive IT investment and coordination. Because IT is such an important part of process investment, the director of information services should be a member of the committee. In fact, it is difficult to imagine the process portfolio being developed and managed without high-level IS involvement. With both information services and human resources management as members, the committee can be the place where people, processes, and technology are incorporated in the investment plan, not simply addressed as peripheral issues later on, with work flows at the center of corporate attention.

In addition to providing a necessary IS perspective on process portfolio decisions, having the IS director on the committee encourages applying a process investment perspective to IT investments. Decisions about information resources, legacy systems, and networks must be made with regard to the processes they support, enable, or create, as well as to the value those processes generate. My hunch is that future developments in IT and its management will make just about all major IT decisions a subset of process investment.

A SENIOR CORPORATE EXECUTIVE

The committee must include one very senior executive who serves as a direct, high-level link to the CEO and ensures the credibility and impact of the committee's work. This person might be the CFO or the chief operating officer. Because process investment will influence the next generation of operations, the COO would be an appropriate choice. I believe only one executive at this level should be part of the committee. In addition to being a poor use of executive time, having two or more with possibly conflicting viewpoints would make them less effective spokespeople for the group's work than a single respected senior executive would be.

THE ROLE OF LONG-TERM PLANNING

Almost every organization has a group whose main responsibility is thinking about and planning for the future. Whether they are called strategic planning or go by some other name, they have a key role to play in business process investment. They can look beyond the current strengths and weaknesses that are likely to absorb the attention of business units and, often, senior managers. Their perspective can help create a portfolio that includes not just the processes that seem to matter today, but also the ones that will matter tomorrow. A strategic planning group that understands the importance of processes can perform four important functions:

- **ANALYZE THE FIRM'S BUSINESS ENVIRONMENT IN PROCESS TERMS.** Again and again, top firms miss the trends that will affect them most because it is so hard for managers to challenge the assumptions that have made them and the company successful. A long-range planning group is in the best position to spot those trends: it is their job to look at the changing outside forces that may make today's process assets tomorrow's liabilities. A firm that has insightful planners *and* listens to them when it is planning process investment has a good chance of avoiding the problems that Sears, IBM, DEC, and other superb firms faced when they ignored changes in their environments and stuck with "tried and true" processes that were being turned into liabilities by their competitors.

- **MOVE THE FIRM AWAY FROM THE LIMITING CONCEPTS OF "THE IN-DUSTRY" AND "CORE PROCESSES."** I've discussed the traditional thinking that prevents firms from accurately judging the salience of some of their processes and blinds them to opportunities for using value builders such as importing and pre-empting to generate new economic value. The perspective of strategic planners and their awareness of the new fluidity of the marketplace should make them advocates for a broader, more creative view of process investment possibilities.

- **LOOK FOR PROCESS PREDATORS.** This is really part of keeping a careful watch on the business environment, but it is important enough to deserve a mention of its own. There is a Dell,

Fidelity, or Wal-Mart in your firm's future. Somewhere a firm is developing new processes or radicalizing old ones in a way that will make them your strongest competitors and may change the rules of competition in your business environment. You'll discount or overlook them because they're not part of your "industry." The most strategic thinkers will look for the early warning signs and help the firm anticipate or quickly respond to such challenges.

- **ENSURE AN EXTENSIVE PROCESS PORTFOLIO.** A strategic planning group that pays attention to changes and potential changes in the business environment and that breaks the bounds of traditional thinking broadens the firm's view of what processes should be part of the portfolio. Thinking about the firm's future viability rather than just its current efficiency and effectiveness will lead planners to (1) protect identity assets; (2) monitor asset depreciation and propose corrective investment; (3) take an enterprise rather than a business unit view and seek opportunities to productize, franchise, and preempt; and (4) look for opportunities for process invention.

THE RIGHT LANGUAGE

Language shapes how we understand reality. Often we do not really see things until we have words to describe them. A new language can provide new perspectives and suggest new kinds of action. While I myself have reservations about many of the fundamental principles of reengineering, I accept that Michael Hammer's popularization of the term created a new way of thinking about business processes. My own—different—conception of business processes as economic assets or liabilities was stimulated by Hammer's language and that of other process movements. So even when I disagree with Hammer, I use his language to help me articulate that disaffection.

In their book *Beyond the Hype,* a team of Harvard Business School researchers reviewed the main trends of management theory and practice as far back as the 1920s. They concluded that very little genuinely new thought has been developed in the years since then. The calls for employee empowerment, decentralization, the breaking down of hierarchies, and other themes that characterize today's business thinking are in fact classic concerns. The ideas are decades old; what has changed is the language used to describe them. They have been repackaged in new words and phrases. The authors argue that this is a strength, not a weakness. The new language gives managers a rhetoric for mobilizing organizations for change.[1] Although the ideas may not be as new as people imagine, talking about them in a new way can create new energy, insight, and shared understanding. A new rallying cry can unify and focus employees and give them a clear sense of purpose, even if it articulates an idea that has been around for awhile.

A vocabulary, new or old, has to be honest to be effective. A corporation whose rhetoric emphasizes the valuing of employees but whose actions communicate the opposite message doesn't fool anyone. *Downsizing* or *rightsizing* are euphemisms that try to gloss over the human pain of slashing costs by cutting jobs and have often been employed by management that does not reduce its own salaries or cut its own jobs in the process. I find that the companies that use clear, direct language to describe the pain associated with cutting costs and improving efficiency are the ones that handle those difficult changes most successfully. Language affects the way we see reality, but it can't blind us to an obvious truth. When managers try to use it for that purpose, it only reduces their credibility and creates additional anger.

The most effective language for mobilizing support for process initiatives and helping to create the conditions for carrying them out successfully will be inclusive and clear. Most process movements have vocabularies that are sometimes unclear and exclusionary or even divisive. TQM, reengineering, and other movements all have their own jargons, and many in effect demand a loyalty oath to a particular narrow concept or ambiguous definition of process. *Reengineering* itself is a term that tends to exclude people, suggesting a focus on improving the machinery of work and the flow of work but ignoring the fact that work is carried out by human beings (whose training and development we don't think of as "reengineering"). The language I use here to describe business process investment is a fairly conservative one, with few new terms. As much as possible, I've drawn on familiar words from business and finance—words whose meanings are generally understood and accepted. Those terms that are new—*identity* versus *priority* versus *background* versus *mandated* processes, for instance—are as clear and commonsensical as I can make them. I've sought to make this language inclusive, limited neither by jargon geared to an elite minority nor by terminology that is narrow and highly specialized. My definition of *process,* for instance, includes many of the activities that other process definitions leave out.

Managers must ensure that participants in business process investment at all levels use the same language for the work they are undertaking and understand it in the same way. Education is thus an important part of an enterprisewide business process investment strategy. Seminars, meetings, newsletters, and other tools are vehicles to develop the common language required for a common effort. If people don't have a shared language, they can't have shared visions, plans, and agendas for action.

CONNECTION AND TRUST

Regardless of differences in strategic styles and change drivers, firms that successfully carry out large-scale process change maintain strong and continuing connection among all levels of the organization. The vision and commitment of senior management can encourage, support, and direct change but can't make it happen. By themselves, top-down directives easily lose momentum and are dissipated as they filter through the firm. If leaders cannot mobilize the talent and commitment of the wider organization, then change programs are almost sure to fail. Too often, top management teams have worked in isolation from the wider organization, operating in virtual secrecy. When and if they do announce "vision statements," their visions are not contagious. General Motors under Roger Smith stands as a sorry contrast to Ford under Don Peterson. Smith was a visionary without followers. Peterson found ways to invite, persuade, and convince people to buy into a vision. Harnessing the energy, knowledge, and cooperation of those on the front lines is essential here. However brilliant the original vision, it cannot be implemented without bottom-up as well as top-down commitment. Middle-out collaboration and team-building are important in bridging the two. "Middle-out collaboration" refers to the actions of supervisors, first-line managers, and mid-level staff who work together to break down functional and departmental barriers and look at process investment needs and process improvement possibilities from an enterprise perspective rather than a local one: division of labor gives way to coordination of knowledge.

The direction, energy, knowledge, and coordination that derive from these parts of the organization must combine into a unified effort to achieve significant change. Communication and, as I've suggested, the language in which communication is carried out are essential tools for establishing that unity of effort. Involving many parts of the organization in planning change is also important. The active presence of business unit leaders, human resources, and IS on the process investment committee is one step toward making the process change program inclusive, not simply a top-down directive or an assortment of local initiatives.

Pluralism—which can be thought of as "empowerment," "the learning organization," or "the death of hierarchy"—helps build a program for change that genuinely involves all levels of the organization. More honored in theory than practice, pluralism means putting decision-making and implementation in the hands of the people who do the work and who usually know more about it than their managers. With appropriate support, education, and incentives from management, employees can build the teams that drive change. Although deciding *which* processes to get right may and perhaps should occur mainly at the top, implementing that choice—determining *how* to get the process right and then doing so—can and should be driven from below.

TRUST

Collaboration does not come easily to Americans. At school we sit at our individual desks and take tests that measure our personal achievement. Collaboration in this setting is usually called cheating. When we are members of teams, it is mainly to compete and win in sports. American individualism is in some ways reinforced by today's economic climate. Downsizing—much of it unfortunately necessary for corporate survival—works against loyalty to the firm: Why be loyal to an organization that may lay you off at any time? And why collaborate in a change program that is likely to involve job losses, possibly including your own? Change that translates into downsizing is more likely to foster a lifeboat mentality, a tendency to protect your own job rather than help others succeed in theirs. These realities interfere with a firm's working together at all levels to bring about change.

Companies that do create or maintain collaborative cultures in such a climate have to work hard to build (or rebuild) employees' trust. Those that succeed in doing so usually do three things well. First, they maintain open communication with the whole firm, providing clear information about what is going on and being honest about the down side as well as the benefits of changes being contemplated. Second, they help the survivors as well as the victims of downsizing or reengineering make the transition to a new situation. It is appropriate that those who lose their jobs receive outplacement services; it is equally appropriate that those who remain be given a clear understanding of how the restructured company will be more effective and how their changed jobs can be satisfying, not just more difficult. Third, the trust-building companies demonstrate their commitment to employees. Investment in employee education is especially important. Motorola is an exemplar, with education the new basis of a mutually beneficial relationship between employer and employee. The Royal Bank of Canada, an outstanding employer for a century, recognizes that, while it can no longer guarantee continuing employment, it can use education and personal development processes to ensure the continued employability of its staff.

INCENTIVES

Process investment that involves significant change is likely to hurt some employees and cause uncertainty for many more. Process change makes some old skills and experience irrelevant; being part of a change team adds work to what is probably an already heavy workload, and some jobs are almost invariably lost. Given these negative inducements, management must provide incentives to encourage employees—people—to be willing participants in change. In practice, unfortunately, changes in incentive systems are usually two years behind a firm's strategic changes.

Education that is of lasting use to employees, whether they remain with the firm or not, is one incentive; empowerment that gives people at many levels real responsibility to manage their own work and participate in setting the future course of the firm is another. Fake empowerment, however, is deadly. Alas, too often reengineering means "you're fired." Be honest and truthful above all. Finally, and most critically, modify performance criteria to reflect the importance of and rewards for creativity, collaboration, and communication. In an era of continuing change and a growing need for teamwork, companies must recognize and reward the qualities that make employees valuable partners in the process investment process.

CHAPTER 10

THE PROCESS INVESTMENT PROCESS

THE PROCESS EDGE IS ABOUT WHAT MANAGERS AND ORGANI-zations must do to plan and carry out successful process investments. In other words, it describes the process investment process. Although the investment process is unlikely to generate economic value directly, its impact on processes that do generate (or drain) value is immense. Skillful investment in the right processes gives a firm a sustained competitive advantage; investing in the wrong processes or managing process change badly can threaten a firm's success or even its survival. For obvious reasons, you should look carefully at your process investment process before using it to make other major business process investments. This chapter brings together the most important principles of my discussion, the ones essential to getting the process investment process right.

I start with a sketch of the typical corporate experience of information services investment over the years, because past errors in IS are so similar to the pitfalls that process investment initiatives face today. Many companies are currently making the same mistakes in business process investment that they made in IS investment in the late 1970s and the 1980s. A brief look at some of the problems that characterized that era illustrates important process investment issues and highlights the value of our process investment principles.

THE LESSONS OF IS INVESTMENT

It is not surprising that there are parallels between process movements in the 1990s and IS movements a decade earlier. The development of information services was, in many ways, the first modern process movement, a fact obscured by the novelty of the technology involved. Because information technology was so new and complex, it was easy for managers to become preoccupied with hardware and software and forget that the aim of information services was to improve business processes. Furthermore, the tensions between discipline and innovation and between central coordination and local action that typified the information services era apply to today's process movements as well.

The early years of information services, dominated by mainframes and monolithic data processing departments, have no equivalent in the process movement era. Once personal computers and local area networks created the possibility of distributing technology throughout the company, however, IS faced situations that are common in the process era.

LACK OF COORDINATION

As the technology became less expensive and more powerful, business units increasingly took charge of their own IT investments. Each IT plan was justified and was developed separately from others in the company. It made use of whatever tools and technology seemed appropriate to local needs. This decentralization of IT decision-making created problems that still dog information services management today: duplication of effort, inconsistent information, and system incompatibility that make it impossible for different areas of the same company to share information. Such patchwork IT environments do not lend themselves to effective hubbing—a serious disadvantage for firms whose competitors can take advantage of more unified (integrated) systems.

The 1990s may well be the period of multi-reengineering chaos, just as the 1980s was the period of multi-technology chaos. Although it is vital that a firm's business units be encouraged to lead process change, a central coordinating mechanism must be established to address shared infrastructures, education, avoidance of redundant work, elimination of incompatibilities, and common goals. To impose some order on IT chaos, many companies have appointed a new style of IS executive, commonly called the chief information officer. Similarly, process movements need both the direction provided by senior management and the perspective of a Gang of X committee to ensure that process change is systematic and organized—a change portfolio, not a grab bag of local projects. This holds true whether particular process innovations are conceived of at the top or on the front lines.

IGNORING PEOPLE

Over the years, countless IS initiatives have focused on technology rather than on the people who use it. Getting the hardware and software up and running was the goal; the technology was considered the source of benefits, and employees were simply expected to adjust themselves to what the machinery required of them. Similarly, firms that undertake major process change tend to concern themselves with work flows rather than the people who do the work. Numerous IT projects are still based on the idea that technology is more important than the technology user, but many IS managers have come to understand that the critical success factors relate to people: their skills and education, the incentives offered them to incorporate new technology in their work, and their belief in the benefits that innovation will create for them and the company.

Human issues have been neglected in the rush to reengineer just as they were in the rush to automate. In this book I've emphasized the importance of looking at people, not work flows. This rule obviously holds true when a firm invests in a people-centered value builder, such as collaboration, but it applies as well to any process change. All business processes depend on people; all process change affects people. Employees involved in the process investment process at all levels need to be listened to, empowered, educated, and rewarded.

LACK OF A GOOD ECONOMIC MODEL

Over the years, IS professionals have put forward various economic justifications for IT spending. During the 1960s and 1970s, they talked about "cost displacement" through IT; in the 1980s, "competitive advantage" was the battle cry. More recently, IS managers have promised dramatic improvements in cost efficiency through client/server computing and through staff reductions made possible by shifting work to computers. Few of these expectations have been fulfilled, and the predicted cost displacement all too rarely occurred. Instead, data management systems generated massive new expenses. The competitive advantage claim has no supporting value metrics: benefits were sometimes exciting, but they almost never generated sustained value for the companies involved. Client/server computing is turning out to be more complex and expensive than most firms expected. It remains to be seen whether downsizing really provides a meaningful economic advantage: in many instances it has not.

As Stephen Roach has pointed out, $100 billion worth of IT investment in the 1980s left worker productivity in financial services essentially unchanged.[1] This productivity paradox has led to some healthy skepticism about IT spending. Part of the chief information officer's job in recent years has been to focus IS efforts on initiatives supported by an economic model based on value created, not benefits. Innovations that provide value directly to the customer are an important target of economically sound IT investment. Numerous studies back Roach's contention that this kind of project does generate meaningful returns. He shows that it took a shift in prioritization from administrative to service systems to resolve the productivity paradox.

The process movement parallel is obvious. Reengineering and other process movement initiatives are too often undertaken without a clear sense of their real cost or their real potential for generating economic value. The result is the process paradox, which, like the productivity paradox, describes dramatic improvements that add no value to the firm and may coincide with or even contribute to corporate decline. There is the danger that information services' history of unfulfilled economic promises is repeating itself in the process era. *The Process Edge* seeks to help firms avoid this hazard. Building a balanced portfolio of process investments with EVA as a guiding economic principle makes creating value the whole focus of process change, not just a hoped-for effect.

ESSENTIAL PRINCIPLES

I have tried to provide a blueprint for successful business process investment in *The Process Edge*. The principles I summarize here are the most important ones—the foundations of its structure. Many of them are implicit in the salience/worth matrix, the essential process investment tool. Apply these essential principles and you will have gone a long way toward ensuring economically sound process investment.

TAKE A BROAD VIEW OF PROCESSES AND PROCESS INVESTMENT

Processes are not just work flows. Soft processes governing decision-making, collaboration, acquisition, research, and many other business activities may be among the most important processes in a firm and the most promising targets for the application of value builders. To be successful, a business process investment strategy must avoid the narrow perspective of many process movements that results in an exclusive focus on work flows and background liabilities. These movements tend to ignore people processes *and* the people who make any process work. I believe that the human dimension of processes and process investment is the most important one. I offer my broad view of what constitutes a process and the openness of the salience/worth matrix to encourage firms to look at all kinds of processes before choosing those that will constitute their process investment portfolios.

A true process investment strategy is a coordinated approach to the process investment portfolio. Concentrating on a single process is unlikely to generate value effectively in a large, complex organization. Giving local initiatives free rein invites the multi-reengineering chaos I described earlier.

In addition to taking a broad view of processes, firms should take a broad, flexible approach to applying process value builders. Although strategic style and change drivers (along with factors in the business environment) powerfully influence a firm's choice, an effective strategy will employ a range of value builders to gain value from a range of processes. The set of value builders I have described can be thought of as "the process investment mutual fund." Although no single firm is likely to invest in all of the funds, managers should be aware of the full range at their disposal.

BE OPEN-MINDED AND IMAGINATIVE ABOUT SALIENCE

Traditional thinking and lack of imagination within a firm can misjudge process salience. Most commonly, CEOs and managers lack the vision to see the potential for greater salience in a supposedly minor process. They miss opportunities to raise process salience in a way that generates new value or provides a new sense of direction to the organization. Notable business successes—for instance, Dell Computer, MCI's "Friends and Family" service, and Federal Express—were the result of imaginative decisions to turn what most firms consider background liability processes into identity assets. Ford's CEO raised the salience of quality processes to give the company a new focus and, in part, a new identity. To a significant degree, process salience is a management choice. USAA chose to make customer contact services its identity processes; other insurance firms see them as priority or background. An airline may choose to make food catering processes priority assets, hoping to attract customers by providing an unusual level or quality and service, or it may see those processes as background liabilities and concentrate on keeping costs down. Thinking imaginatively about process salience has the potential to create new sources of value.

The salience of processes can also be affected by changes outside the firm. Dell treated forecasting and product development as background processes, but rapid improvements in computer technology and changing customer demands raised the salience of those processes, making them essential to the company's future viability. They became priority processes whether Dell wanted them to or not. Managers who are determining process salience must always take their business environments into account and look for trends or developments that raise or lower the salience of their existing processes.

THINK PROCESS WORTH AND EVA

Defining process worth in economic terms is the heart of business process investment. Processes are assets if they add economic value to a firm and liabilities if they drain it. Value-preserving and option-enabling processes may also be considered assets because they maintain a firm's current ability to generate value and ensure its future ability to do so, although they may not create economic value directly. Process worth is a fundamental concept too often ignored by process movement advocates. Evaluating process improvements in terms of their potential to create value is the only way to judge if investing in them makes economic sense. Thinking in terms of process benefits rather than value invites the process paradox, either because the benefits are not germane to how the organization creates value or because the cost of achieving those benefits is greater than their economic value. Hence the importance of EVA. Because it is a determination of added value after the cost of the capital used to generate it has been taken into account, it is the most reliable measure of whether investment in process change actually increases the firm's economic value.

In determining the EVA of process improvement, it is essential to base your calculations on the true capital cost of change, which is often higher than typical corporate estimates. The often overlooked costs of education, support, severance pay, facilities, management time, and a range of corporate overhead costs must be taken into account. This is not to say that managers need to figure either costs or potential value to the penny. In most cases, accurate detailed calculations are not possible, as accounting systems are not designed to reflect the economic realities of processes. A reasonable estimate based on a solid understanding of the *capital* tied up in processes and needed for value builders is not only sufficient but infinitely preferable to superficially precise figures showing process *expenses*.

If you don't fool yourself, your investors won't be fooled. When IT gurus lauded American Hospital Supply, Merrill Lynch, McKesson, and Citibank for the competitive advantages they had achieved through innovative IT initiatives, the stock prices of those firms did not rise significantly. Investors understood that IT benefits were not the same as economic benefits. State-of-the-art technology was less important than the facts that Merrill Lynch failed to keep costs under control, McKesson overpaid for acquisitions, and Citibank overpaid for market share and failed to manage its exposure to risk well. During the same period, Wal-Mart's stock did go up, not because it made brilliant use of information technology (although it did), but because its innovations generated an economic value that investors could see and measure.

PROTECT IDENTITY ASSET PROCESSES

As my many examples have made clear, identity asset processes distinguish a firm from its competitors. McDonald's quality and consistency, Federal Express's on-time delivery, and Sony's product innovations draw customers and investors; they are prime sources of company value. Firms that do not have identity asset processes and must compete on the basis on their priority processes are likely to be constantly on the defensive. Lacking distinctive processes and a distinctive identity, the most they can hope for is to keep a little ahead of the pack. They can be only "me too" competitors. Every firm's business process investment strategy must include looking carefully at identity processes to judge whether investment in them can create new economic opportunities or protect existing value.

Like any other asset, identity processes tend to depreciate.

They need continual maintenance, enhancement, and review. Processes have natural life cycles, and identity assets can lose value or become liabilities in various ways:

- Competitors replicate the process, turning it into a commodity

- Customers and investors cease to see an old identity process as providing a desirable product or service that is worth their purchase or investment

- The firm freezes the process, failing to make adjustments required by a changing environment

- A competitor invents a new process that decreases the value of the process or changes the rules of competition

These conditions can affect any process, but the damage is obviously greatest when an identity process is weakened. Effective business process investment means strengthening identity processes, being alert to external changes that may threaten them, and, in some cases, being open to developing new identity processes.

CONTINUALLY IMPROVE PRIORITY ASSET PROCESSES

I sense in my own work as a consultant with companies and in the thinking and research that led to *The Process Edge* that identity process assets are the fundamental base of new competition. There are fewer and fewer sustainable product advantages, fewer and fewer protected market advantages, and fewer and fewer national advantages. That means there are fewer and fewer ways of creating and sustaining market differentiation. I can't see any way of making a firm stand out other than by process, except in the rare cases in which there's a patent advantage. Identity process assets are, then, literally the capital of the firm: the knowledge processes of IBM, the customer service processes of USAA, the logistical processes of Federal Express, the development processes of Microsoft. I hope that my book raises a question that will worry and energize managers: What are our identity asset processes?

Priority processes support identity processes and determine the quality and metrics of current performance. When priority processes decline or fail, the effects are quickly apparent to customers

and investors. When they are executed outstandingly well, they create and maintain a firm's reputation for consistent excellence. The
word *priority* itself suggests the essential role these processes play.
A firm whose priority processes are liabilities is in serious trouble.
Because successful operation depends on priority processes, maintaining their quality is a requisite of continued competitiveness;
improving them can generate considerable value. A 5 percent supe-
riority translates to industry dominance. And a 5 percent inferior-
ity translates to disaster.

In successful firms, priority processes will necessarily be assets.
This means they will probably be ignored by reengineering gurus
like Hammer and Champy, who focus on broken processes and
propose radical, risky programs to fix them. But I believe that
assets provide major opportunities for investment without the
uncertainty and stress of radical change. Although less dramatic
than wholesale reengineering, improving priority assets continually
and incrementally over time can have results that are just as far-
reaching but also more likely to generate real value. McDonald's
commitment to making its priority asset processes a little better
every year has helped it maintain its dominance in an extremely
competitive environment.

Although TQM is only one of many approaches to process
improvement, it is a natural choice for much priority asset investment, with its emphasis on making viable processes steadily better
over a long period of time. TQM, with most other process movements, has also emphasized the importance of focusing on the customer—an important antidote to the tendency of companies to
organize processes around their own priorities, assumptions, and
operating needs.

OUTSOURCE BACKGROUND AND MANDATED LIABILITIES

Again, I urge managers to avoid the pitfall of investing heavily
in background processes simply because their work flows are
so obviously fixable or because these are the processes that are
most visible through the lens of reengineering. Although handling
background processes badly can mean value loss, handling them

superbly well seldom results in a significant payoff. Expensive and stressful change programs that are limited to background liabilities are unlikely to add value to a company. I recommend that background liability processes (and mandated processes, which are almost always liabilities) be outsourced whenever possible; in most cases, this will reduce the capital tied up in them. Equally important (and an argument for outsourcing even when it does not lower capital costs) is that outsourced background liabilities no longer divert the management time and attention that should be given to identity and priority processes.

The key, remember, is to outsource your background processes to firms for whom these processes are identity assets. To my earlier example of Laura Ashley outsourcing its distribution processes to Business Logistics, I add one from Tom Peters's personal experience. In *The Tom Peters Seminar: Crazy Times Call for Crazy Organizations,* he describes speaking at a large Marriott hotel where the car parking valets did such an excellent job that he mentioned them at the end of his speech and said, "Hats off to Marriott." A member of the audience identified himself as co-owner of Professional Parking Services, the firm that Marriott contracts with for valet parking. Peters comments: "Regardless of the job, from car parking to biochemical research, there are folks out there who sweat the narrow task as if it were a matter of life or death (which it is for them). I have trouble getting excited about parking, and I expect that Marriott's hotel managers, their platters already balanced with a thousand hot dishes, do, too. But to Paul Paliska and his brother Stephen, parking is a passion. . . . And passion makes perfect."[2]

GET THE WHOLE ORGANIZATION ON BOARD

My chapter on building an enterprise strategy makes clear that process investment cannot be successfully carried out in isolation by either the corporate leadership or those on the front lines. Except in extremely rare cases, even visionary CEOs need the insights and experience of the managers who make up my proposed Gang of X to help them formulate an effective process portfolio and strategy. In similar fashion, change initiatives developed by individual managers without direction from the top are likely to focus too much on local concerns (usually background liabilities). And without the commitment and understanding of employees at all levels, effective change is not possible.

So a key part of the process investment process is making it a unified effort. The tools to build unity of purpose include

- education that establishes a common language for change and a common understanding of what changes are planned and why they are desirable;
- openness and honesty about change to help foster an atmosphere of trust; and
- incentives at all levels so that those who make change happen can have a reasonable expectation of benefiting from it.

REMEMBER THAT MEANINGFUL CHANGE TAKES TIME

Process investment, like other forms of capital investment, is investment in the future. In most cases, the economic value it generates comes over time. Process investment is not about quick fixes or financial windfalls. Management that is generally willing to wait as long as five years to realize returns on traditional capital investments should have the same expectations for the capital invested in processes. Few, if any, of the process successes described in this book were overnight triumphs. Most required the persistence of leadership that kept the organization clearly focused on a specified goal over the course of several years.

Change is not easy. Any significant modification of a company calls for the planning and coordination of many complex processes; more important, it requires the cooperation of affected employees, whether they design, manage, or implement the changes. Crash programs characterized by stress and uncertainty are not known for generating companywide trust and cooperation. Although the pace of business change often demands corporate agility and responsiveness, the most successful process strategies are based on long-term goals and try to anticipate environmental changes rather than hurriedly react to them.

The need to keep the market happy is not a valid excuse for corporate shortsightedness. Despite all the attention given to the market's supposed emphasis on short-term gains, ample evidence shows that most investors look at the long-term value of companies, not just this quarter's earnings. Process investment that adds value over time—and is seen by stockholders to add value—is the best guarantor of market success.

IN CONCLUSION: START WITH THE RIGHT QUESTIONS

Although the process investment techniques described in *The Process Edge* may be new to many readers, they are based on well-established principles of economic value and on a flexible, commonsense approach to understanding an organization's processes and deciding how to invest in them. Creating an effective processes investment process takes planning and effort, but it is not an arcane science. It is mainly a matter of asking and answering some basic, essential questions about your company's processes:

- Do we know what our identity and priority processes are?
- Do we know if they are assets or liabilities?
- Are we overlooking processes that don't fit neatly into a concept of processes as work flows?
- Are we overinvesting in improving background liability processes, or do we have a balanced portfolio of process investments?
- Could some of our processes create new value if we make them more important (raise their salience)?
- Do we have a true sense of the capital tied up in our important processes?
- Do we know our firm's cost of capital?
- Can we accurately estimate the true cost of the value builders we plan to apply?
- Do we have ways of measuring process value (and not just process benefits)?

Managers should be able to answer or find the answers to all these questions, because they address the most fundamental issues of how companies operate and how they create value that is recognized by customers and stockholders. These questions reflect a down-to-earth, commonsense strategy for determining which business processes deserve investment and what form that investment should take. Getting the right process right is the key to achieving a process edge.

NOTES

CHAPTER 1

1. Gene Hall, Jim Rosenthal, and Judy Wade, "How to Make Reengineering *Really* Work," *Harvard Business Review,* November–December 1993, 119.

2. S. S. Roach, *Technology and the Service Sector: America's Hidden Challenge* (Morgan Stanley Special Economic Study, Technical Report, 1987).

3. Going as far back as the eighteenth century, in *Mastering the Dynamics of Innovation* (Boston: Harvard Business School Press, 1994) James Utterback tracks the development of ice-making, light bulbs, personal computer hardware, typewriters, and rayon. He divides the history of these products into "fluid," "transitional," and "specific" phases. The fluid phase is one of dramatic innovation and competition among designs. In the transitional phase, one design becomes dominant. A dominant design—for instance, the screw-in lightbulb, the IBM personal computer, the QWERTY keyboard, or the Microsoft Windows operating system—is one that captures the marketplace and sets the rules to which competitors, suppliers, and secondary producers must adapt if they are to survive. Its success is followed by a rapid sorting out of industry competitors, with many of them abandoning the industry altogether. Such standardization leads to fierce price competition and turns innovative products into commodities: this is the specific phase. When success depends on providing a specific product-commodity to a market niche at high levels of efficiency, the focus of innovation shifts from product to process.

4. Pauline Graham, ed., *Mary Parker Follett—Prophet of Management: A Celebration of Writings from the 1920s* (Boston: Harvard Business School Press, 1995).

5. Peter F. Drucker, *Landmarks of Tomorrow* (New York: Harper, 1959), 53.

6. Henry J. Johanssen et al., *Business Process Re-Engineering: Breakpoint Strategies for Market Dominance* (New York: John Wiley and Sons, 1993), 42.

7. David J. Teece, Gary Pisano, and Amy Shuen, "Dynamic Capabilities and Strategic Management," unpublished manuscript, University of California at Berkeley, reviewed in June 1992.

8. C. I. Baldwin and K. B. Clark, "Capabilities and Capital Investment: New Perspectives on Capital Budgeting," Working Paper 92-004, Harvard Business School, Boston, 1992.

9. Jeffrey Pfeffer, *Competitive Advantage through People: Unleashing the Power of the Work Force* (Boston: Harvard Business School Press, 1994), 3.

10. Ibid., 4.

11. T. W. Malone, "What Is Coordination Theory?" Working Paper 2051-88, MIT Sloan School of Management, Cambridge, Mass., 1988.

12. Fernando Flores, *Offering New Principles for a Shifting Business World* (Belmont, Calif.: Business Design Associates, 1991), 21.

13. Ronald H. Coase, "The Nature of the Firm," in *The Nature of the Firm: Origins, Evolution, and Development,* eds. Oliver E. Williamson and Sidney G. Winter (New York: Oxford University Press, 1993), ch. 2.

14. M. S. Scott Morton, *The Corporation of the 1990s* (Oxford: Oxford University Press, 1991), 8.

15. Paul Ingrassia and Joseph B. White, *Comeback: The Fall and Rise of the American Automobile Industry* (New York: Simon & Schuster, 1994).

16. This article was quoted without citation on the Internet. (The Internet, while providing access to vast amounts of information, makes it difficult to attribute original sources.)

17. Peter Drucker, "A Cantankerous Interview with Peter Schwartz and Kevin Kelly," *Wired,* August 1996, 179–185.

18. Shawn Tully, "The Real Key to Creating Wealth," *Fortune,* 20 September 1993, 38–50.

CHAPTER 2

1. As this book was going to press, I came across these figures in Bruce Upbin's "Annual Report on American Industry" (*Forbes,* 13 January 1997, 122 and 249): of the 1,000 largest U.S. companies, Dell and Compaq rank tenth and twenty-second, respectively. Within the corporate and communication industry, *Forbes* ranks Dell and Compaq second and third in their five-year average return on capital and ranks Dell the number one company in 1996 for return on equity. Interestingly, the only company to surpass Dell and Compaq in its five-year average return on capital is Gateway 2000, the mail-order company that copied Dell's identity process.

CHAPTER 3

1. Thomas H. Davenport, *Process Innovation: Reengineering Work through Information Technology* (Boston: Harvard Business School Press, 1993), 28.

2. Michael Hammer and James Champy, *Reengineering the Corporation: A Manifesto for Business Revolution* (New York: Harper Business, 1993).

3. *Management processes* include vision-setting and leadership, sales force incentives and rewards, account management, business area management, public relations, internal communications, and economic and industry forecasting. *Manufacturing processes* include quality management, capacity planning, production planning, inventory control, procurement, and distribution. *Marketing processes* include pricing, advertising, channel selection and management, product announcement, customer events and surveys, and consumer marketing. *Educational processes* include internal skill dynamics, customer education, and management development. *Technology development processes* include research and design, technology evaluation, new-product selection, standards-setting, joint venture development, testing, and project management. *Financial processes* include budgeting, foreign exchange, investment planning, performance reporting, investor relations, leasing, credit management, facilities management, divestment of business units, and cash management. *Organizational processes* include human resources planning, downsizing and early retirement programs, recruitment, performance evaluation, and promotion. *Legal processes* include regulatory compliance, patents, and safety. *Alliance processes* include the IBM business partners program and other joint ventures. *Sales processes* include direct marketing, contracting, and branch management. *Customer support processes* include systems engineering, technical support, facilities management, warranties, and repairs. *Product line and line of business management processes* include personal computers, client/server computing, AS/400, RS/6000, mainframes, network products, database management, object-oriented tools, consulting, and outsourcing. The brochure is available from Andersen Consulting, Chicago.

4. S. Jones, "Digital Retools," *Information Week*, 1994.

5. Hammer and Champy, *Reengineering the Corporation*, 35.

CHAPTER 4

1. Paul Strassman, one of the great intellects in the management field, effectively debunks claims for the value of such soft benefits made by IT gurus. He addresses the subject in *Information Payoff* and in a chapter of *Measuring Business Value of Information Technologies,* as well as in many articles.

2. I use the phrase "direct attributable expense" rather than "direct expense" to avoid potential confusion created by the accounting distinction between direct and indirect costs.

3. For a more detailed discussion of hidden IT expenses, see "The Economics of Information Capital" in my book *Shaping the Future: Business Design through Information Technology* (Boston: Harvard Business School Press, 1991). The statistics presented here come largely from that book. They have been confirmed by other studies and surveys.

4. Alfred Rappaport, *Creating Shareholder Value: The New Standard for Business Performance* (New York: The Free Press, 1986), 13.

5. "A Personal Interview with Peter Drucker," *Reengineering Quarterly* (February 1995).

6. G. Bennett Stewart, III, *The Quest for Value: The EVA Management Guide* (New York: Harper Business, 1991), 193.

7. If your friend told you he would finance an investment by not paying his credit card that particular month, then his cost of capital is the interest rate on the credit card debt. This is his "opportunity cost," money or real cost to him even though he didn't hand over a check. The core of EVA at the corporate level is calculated by the investor's opportunity cost of equity. For a fuller discussion, see Stewart, *The Quest for Value,* which I strongly recommend for readers interested in the mechanics of this very complex subject; I also recommend *Valuation: Measuring and Managing the Values of Companies,* by Tom Copeland, Tim Koller, and Jack Murrin (New York: John Wiley and Sons, 1995).

8. Shawn Tully, "The Real Key to Creating Wealth," *Fortune,* 20 September 1993, 40.

9. I looked at eight leading books on reengineering and found that none has a chapter on economics or investment or lists the word "capital" in the index. The leading book in the field does not deal with the subject of economic value at all. One of the books had a paragraph that mentions economic change as one of the forces driving the need for process breakthroughs. Another had a single page on "cost-benefit analysis" that defined costs only in terms of expenses. Only one of the books considers value metrics and discusses the cost and sources of funding process improvements. It also mentions—briefly—that the improvements should lead to measurable benefits for customers *and* shareholders.

10. See Stan Davis and Bill Davidson, *20/20 Vision: Transform Your Business Today to Succeed in Tomorrow's Economy* (New York: Simon & Schuster, 1991); George Stalk, Jr., and Thomas M. Hout, *Competing Against Time: How Time-Based Competition Is Reshaping Global Markets* (New York: The Free Press, 1990); and Peter G. W. Keen, *Competing in Time* (Cambridge, Mass.: Ballinger Publishing Company, 1988).

11. Stewart, *The Quest for Value,* 23.

12. Tully, "The Real Key to Creating Wealth," 38.

13. Ibid., 40.

14. Ibid.

15. Ibid. and personal communication.

CHAPTER 5

1. Personal communication.

2. Workstations can be thought of as souped-up PCs designed to operate at high speeds and handle multiple tasks concurrently. When a customer service agent is, for instance, entering a loan applicant's information at his or her workstation, the system simultaneously accesses the relevant credit records. As PCs become more and more powerful, the distinction between PC and workstation is breaking down. Both workstations and the most advanced PCs can be thought of as stations for information- and communications-centered work.

3. Personal communication. See also Arno Penzias, *Harmony* (New York: Harper Business, 1995).

4. Juliette Shor, *Overworked Americans: The Unexpected Decline of Leisure* (New York: Basic Books, 1993).

5. Keen, *Competing in Time,* 95.

CHAPTER 6

1. The integration of separate IT systems involves complex technical challenges, some of which may be insurmountable today. Until recently, the computer and telecommunications industries were dominated by proprietary systems: supplier-specific formats, interfaces, procedures, and languages that do not mesh with one another. Although new systems are usually "open"—based on standards that allow them to communicate with one another—we are still a long way from having open systems as the norm. Legacy systems are almost all proprietary.

2. Peter G. W. Keen and J. Michael Cummins, *Networks in Action* (Belmont, Calif.: Wadsworth Publishers, 1994), 168–169.

3. *Offering Principles for a Shifting Business World* (Alameda, Calif.: Business Design Associates, 1992).

4. Michael Schrage, *No More Teams* (New York: Currency Doubleday, 1990).

5. Digital Equipment Corporation, Internal company newsletter, 1991.

6. Schrage, *No More Teams.*

7. Shoshona Zuboff, *In the Age of the Smart Machine: The Future of Work and Power* (New York: Basic Books, 1988).

CHAPTER 7

1. When the Bell system was split up, AT&T contracted with regional Bell companies to handle call accounting at the sender's end. Because the local company's phone switch cannot access information from the switch at the receiver's end directly, AT&T's accounting system cannot identify who is being called as readily as MCI's.

2. Shoshona Zuboff interview in *Decisions* 3 (1993).

3. Richard T. Pascale, *Managing on the Edge: How the Smartest Companies Use Conflict to Stay Ahead* (New York: Simon & Schuster, 1990), 16–17.

4. *Economist,* 20 July 1996.

5. *Forbes,* 16 September 1994.

CHAPTER 8

1. Henry J. Johanssen et al., *Business Process Re-Engineering: Breakpoint Strategies for Market Dominance* (New York: John Wiley and Sons, 1993), ch. 1.

2. Even amid the political, economic, and social turmoil created by the misdeeds of the Carlos Salinas de Gortari presidency, the two firms I worked with continued to thrive. More than 80 percent of their top management have degrees in business, engineering, or economics from Stanford, Harvard, Berkeley, and the like. They are aware of the importance of process advantages and know that no economy can succeed purely on the basis of low labor costs.

3. "Reengineering IS," *CIO Magazine,* June 1995.

4. "Annual Survey," *Fortune,* February 1995.

CHAPTER 9

1. Robert G. Eccles and Nitin Nohria with James D. Berkley, *Beyond the Hype* (Boston: Harvard Business School Press, 1992), 17–37.

CHAPTER 10

1. S. S. Roach, "Organization Characteristics and MIS Success in the Context of Small Business," *MIS Quarterly* 9, no. 1 (March 1985).

2. Tom Peters, *The Tom Peters Seminar: Crazy Times Call for Crazy Organizations* (New York: Vintage Press, 1994), 138–139.

INDEX

ABOUT THE AUTHOR

Peter G. W. Keen is the author of fifteen books on the link between information technology and business strategy, an international adviser to top managers, named by *Information Week* as one of the top ten consultants in the world, and a professor who has held positions at leading U.S. and European universities, including Harvard, Stanford, MIT, and Stockholm University. Companies with which Keen has worked on an ongoing, long-term basis include British Airways, Citibank, MCI Communications, Sweden Post, Cemex (Mexico), and the Royal Bank of Canada. All of his work focuses on bridging the worlds, cultures, and language of business and IT.